D1496344

Jean Baptiste Le Moyne de Bienville

Louisiana Life Series No. 10

Bienville
Father of Louisiana

by
Philomena Hauck

Published by
The Center for Louisiana Studies
University of Southwestern Louisiana

Library of Congress Number: 98-73813
ISBN Number: 1-887366-25-3

Published by The Center for Louisiana Studies
P.O. Box 40831
University of Southwestern Louisiana
Lafayette, LA 70504-0831

Contents

I. Beginnings 1

II. A Colony is Founded 9

III. Bienville's First Administration 24

IV. Trials and Conflicts 45

V. The Crozat Regime 55

VI. John Law Makes an Impression 67

VII. An Influx of Settlers 80

VIII. The Company Tightens its Hold 92

IX. Bienville in France 102

X. Périer at the Helm 106

XI. Bienville Returns 116

XII. The Second Chickasaw War 126

XIII. Bienville's Last Years 137

XIV. Conclusion 140

Appendix 143

Bibliographic Essay 148

Index 152

Bienville
Father of Louisiana

Chapter I
Beginnings

During the French regime in North America, the Le Moyne clan was a force to be reckoned with. From Newfoundland to Hudson Bay and from Quebec to Louisiana, Le Moynes were everywhere, battling the enemies of France and extending the borders of the French empire in the New World. But they were peacemakers too, with a talent for forest diplomacy. At critical moments in French-Indian relations, a Le Moyne could parley with native chiefs in their own language, using their own lofty rhetoric until an agreement was hammered out and the peace pipe was passed around. And if there was often guile on both sides, there was respect, even a certain warmth, as well. The most famous of this remarkable family was Pierre Le Moyne d'Iberville who performed miracles of heroism before his untimely death in Havana at the age of forty-five. Far less flamboyant than his older brother, Jean-Baptiste Le Moyne de Bienville, commonly known simply as Bienville, also made an enduring name for himself. Left in charge of the infant colony of Louisiana at the age of twenty-two and virtually abandoned by the French authorities, he managed to hold his own against suspicious Spaniards on the one flank and aggressive English colonists on the other. Today he is honored as the founder of New Orleans and the father of Louisiana.

Jean-Baptiste was the twelfth child in a family of twelve boys and two girls born to Charles Le Moyne and his wife Catherine Thierry. In the sparsely populated colony that came to be known as Canada, large families like the Le Moynes were nothing out of the ordinary. Bachelors were subtly—and not so subtly—encouraged to marry, and when they did settle down, the king of France made it worth their while to have plenty of children. At his birth, Bienville brought his father the customary bonus of 400 *livres* a year awarded to parents of twelve or more children. Since no such statistics were kept in those days, Bienville's exact birth date is unknown, but parish records tell us that Jean-Baptiste Le Moyne was baptized in the Church of St. Joseph in Montreal on February 23, 1680, which would probably have been a day or two after his birth. The landed title of Bienville came to him ten years later from an older brother of that name who was killed in a skirmish with the Iroquois.

Bienville spent the first eighteen years of his life in Canada, where he acquired beliefs and attitudes that lasted throughout his long career. His tenacity, his talent for keeping the native tribes in the French interest, and his sure sense of when to be bold and when to be cautious, all these were lessons which he learned on the Canadian frontier, particularly from his father and his older brothers.

By the time Bienville was born, his father was no longer plain Charles Le Moyne, but the Sieur de Longueuil et de Chateauguay. Over the years he had been awarded huge tracts of land and a patent of nobility for his services to his country in peace and war. In addition, he had amassed a considerable fortune from his fur trading business, and his stone house at the corner of St. Joseph and St. Paul Street in Montreal was the finest the little colony could boast of.

Everything Charles Le Moyne owned he had earned the hard way. He was born in Dieppe, France, in 1626, the son of a local innkeeper. In the class-ridden society of the day, where an idle count without a brain in his head could lord it over the worthiest commoner, an innkeeper's son was just another nobody, born to live and die in obscurity. Noble lineage was everything, a passport to fame and advancement. Of course a young man with a hankering for a more adventurous life could emigrate to France's new colony in North America—as long as he was willing to risk his life in the process. It so happened that Charles Le Moyne's uncle, Adrien Duchesne, who was a surgeon in the colony, offered to advance passage money to Charles and his brother Jacques. The offer was accepted, and in due course the two boys crossed the Atlantic to seek their fortunes in the New World.

At the time, Canada, then known as New France, was little more than a fur trading center with a population of about 350 souls scattered throughout a few tiny settlements along the St. Lawrence River. The colony was leased to the Company of New France which had undertaken to bring out 200 settlers a year and foot the bill for administrative expenses in return for a monopoly on the fur trade. But settlement was slow. With the tools then available, it took more than a year of backbreaking labor to clear an acre of ground in the dense forests of Quebec, and a year or two more for the stumps to rot before crops could be planted. Although tiny patches of cultivated land were beginning to appear among the forests of oak, pine, and maple, fur was still the lifeblood of the colony. It was the beaver trade which allowed the settlers to buy a few necessities from France and enabled the Company to meet expenses and hopefully make a profit.

After his arrival in Canada, the fifteen-year-old Charles Le Moyne spent four years working for the Jesuits at their mission to the Hurons on the eastern shore of Georgian Bay. In Huronia, the new recruit learned how to survive in the wilderness, how to hunt and fish and snowshoe, and how to maneuver a frail birch bark canoe as well as any Indian. Living with the native people as closely as he did, he became familiar with their languages and their ways, and they came to know and trust him. He also forged lifelong bonds of respect for the Jesuit priests, who were willing to risk their lives in well-meaning, but ultimately not very successful efforts to convert the native people. He could see that the priests performed many useful functions other than preaching the Gospel. They did their best to prevent greedy fur-traders from cheating the Indians; and seeing the terrible effects that a jug or two of alcohol had on the unfortunate natives who had no previous experience with liquor of any kind, the priests did everything possible to keep it out of Indian villages. By mastering Indian languages and adapting themselves to Indian ways, the priests also extended French influence in village after village. For all these reasons, Charles Le Moyne and his sons were convinced that the Jesuits made the best missionaries and diplomats, and this partiality for the order was to cause Bienville a lot of grief in Louisiana.

Meanwhile, following a four-year stint in Huronia, Charles Le Moyne was given the job of storekeeper and interpreter at Trois Rivières, after which he was sent to Montreal, the most dangerous outpost in the colony.

Strange as it may seem to the modern mind, Montreal had been established for religious reasons. Intended to be the center of a mission to the Indians, it was founded by Paul Chomedy de Maisonneuve four years before Le Moyne's arrival. The governor of the day, Houalt de Montmagny, was opposed to the venture. Not that the governor was displeased to see fifty new settlers in the colony; but to choose the island of Montreal, right in the jaws of the hostile Iroquois[1] was sheer madness, as far as he was concerned. Nonetheless, Maisonneuve held his ground, vowing that he would go there even if every tree on the island were to be changed into an Iroquois.

Just as Montmagny had predicted, the little contingent barely had time to settle in before the attacks commenced. In all fairness, the Iroquois attacks on Montreal were not out of innate ferocity, as some people would have it, but out of a need for furs. For several years, the Iroquois, who lived in present-day New York State and southern Ontario, had been bartering furs for English and Dutch trade goods, while the Hurons were allies and trading partners of the French. By the 1640s, furs in Iroquois hunting grounds—never very plentiful to begin with—were almost exhausted and the Indians faced disaster. To obtain the hatchets, kettles, and guns they could no longer do without, they had to have access to new hunting grounds. Blocking the route to the rich northern forests were the Hurons, enemies of the Iroquois for as long as man could remember. Initially the Iroquois tried to win a share of the Huron fur trade by negotiation and when this failed they turned to war. As soon as they found out about Maisonneuve's new settlement at the junction of the two great waterways to the interior, the Ottawa and the St. Lawrence rivers, they set out to destroy it. Masters of ambushing techniques, Iroquois attackers hid

[1]The Iroquois Confederacy consisted of five tribes. From east to west they were as follows: Mohawks, Oneidas, Onondagas, Cayugas, and Senecas.

behind trees and lurked between buildings, pouncing on anyone who dared to venture beyond the fort. In these grim years, everyone had to be a hero to survive. Even the women showed their mettle. Priest-historian, Dollier de Casson, has an anecdote about one redoubtable "amazon" as he called her, named Catherine Primot, whose daughter later married Charles Le Moyne. Surprised by a marauding Iroquois brave, she saved herself from being scalped by grabbing her assailant in a place which, as De Casson delicately puts it, "modesty forbids me to relate."

From first to last Charles Le Moyne played such a bold part in defending the colony that he became recognized as a hero among heroes. As well as repelling several attacks, he led many a foray against the Iroquois until his luck finally ran out and he was captured in an ambush. Montrealers feared the worst:

> No doubt was felt that he had been most cruelly burnt, since for a long time they [the Iroquois] had all tried hard to catch him and so placate the appetites of their old men who for several years had gathered together wood from time to time to burn him. . . .[2]

Typically, Le Moyne kept his wits about him. Speaking in their own language, he warned his captors of the terrible revenge that would be exacted on their whole nation if they dared to kill him. The upshot was that they released him to some friendly Indians who took him back to Montreal.

Charles Le Moyne lived to take part in several more campaigns against the Iroquois. Between raising his large family and defending the colony, he also became a successful fur-trader and landowner. Worn out before his time with all his exertions he died in 1685 when Bienville was only five years old, and his wife followed him to the grave five years later. As a matter of course, the bulk of his estate, including the large *seigneurie*[3] of Longueuil near Montreal, went to his oldest son Charles, with small legacies to each of the other children.

After his father's death, Bienville was raised by his eldest brother Charles, Sieur de Longueuil, later Baron de Longueuil. From an early age, he must have known that he belonged to a very special family. His father's exploits were the stuff of legend and his older brothers were all making names for themselves in the field and in the council chamber. By the standards of the day, the Longueuil *seigneurie* was quite remarkable, with its fine stone buildings, surrounded by high walls to protect the settlers from hostile incursions. Governor Louis de Buade, Comte de Frontenac,

[2]Dollier de Casson, *A History of Montreal, 1640-1672*. Edited and translated by Ralph Flenley (Toronto, 1928), 131-33.

[3]The name given to an estate owned by a member of the landed gentry.

who was not in the habit of praising anybody's possessions except his own, wrote that it reminded him of one of the fortified castles of France. But of far greater significance to Bienville in the long run than family possessions was the confidence that came from belonging to an exceptionally close knit family who could always count on one another for support and advancement.

Very likely Bienville was educated by the Sulpician priests who ran the only boys' school in Montreal. Housed in a two-room building on Notre Dame Street, the school probably taught basic reading, writing, arithmetic, as well as the principles of the Catholic religion. Judging by his correspondence, Bienville knew how to marshall an argument and he could express himself vigorously, but he was certainly no scholar. More valuable than formal schooling was the practical education he received on the Canadian frontier. It goes without saying that he spent much of his time outdoors like other Canadian youths, hunting, fishing, and trekking around his brother's broad acres. While still young, he learned to negotiate a flimsy birchbark canoe through shoals and across rapids, always on the alert for possible snipers lurking along the banks. And when his brothers gathered in the Longueuil *château*, he learned more about military tactics and native diplomacy than he could ever find in books. He also came to know the colonial notables, from the governor down, who might visit Longueuil on their way to or from Montreal.

Montreal was an exciting place to grow up in, sometimes too exciting for the clergy and the local authorities. By this time Maisonneuve's pious settlement had lost much of its early fervor. It was a noisy, bustling place with a population of about 1,000 souls and a large floating population. Priests, soldiers, explorers, fur-traders, and native people all rubbed shoulders together on the narrow streets, attending to business, or perhaps lurching from one of the numerous taverns before heading for the canoes that would take them to Quebec or to the West. In spring the *coureurs de bois*[4] paddled from Montreal to the *pays d'en haut*[5] with their guns, hatchets, and knives—and unfortunately their brandy—and returned in the fall with cargoes of fur, and perhaps with some information about far-off tribes. Their furs sold, as likely as not they blew their profits in one spree after another before setting out for the wilderness the following year. Although the bulk of the fur-trading was carried on in the western posts, some native traders still paddled down to Montreal every spring, set up their tepees on the Common, kindled their fires, and unpacked their wares for prospective

[4]Unlicensed fur traders who scattered into the woods in search of furs, traded in brandy, and shared the nomadic ways of the native people.

[5]The high country, i.e., the wilderness.

buyers. It was also to Montreal that delegations of native chieftains made annual visits to meet the governor general of the day to give him a kind of state of the union message and recount any grievances they might have against dishonest traders or against their enemies, the Iroquois. Surrounded by his train of officers, and perhaps a Le Moyne for interpreter, the governor made a gracious speech in reply. As was customary on those occasions, he concluded by expressing his love for his "children" and his concern for their welfare. The chiefs probably took some of these fine sentiments with a grain of salt, for most of them had undoubtedly seen enough governors come and go to know that these fine gentlemen were not in the habit of allowing the welfare of their "children" to stand in the way of France's strategic interests. For all that, the Indians had a certain affection for the French that they never had for the English because the French treated them with more tact and consideration—although our admiration for Gallic *bonhomie* should perhaps be tempered by the knowledge that the French needed Indian cooperation more than the English did. The very existence of the French colony rested not on farming as did the English colonies, but on the fur trade, which depended on Indian goodwill. This talent for getting along with the native people stood Bienville in good stead in Louisiana, where he managed to rally the tribes to the French side, even when it might have been in their own best interest to defect.

It goes without saying that the young man was proud of his French heritage, yet in every bone of his sturdy body he was very different from the native-born Frenchman. These second-generation Canadians, particularly those living in and around Montreal who were in constant association with the native people, were an entirely new breed. Tough, hardy, and self-reliant, they matched their Indian neighbors in courage, and resourcefulness. Whereas a native Frenchman might live a lifetime without travelling beyond his own village, a Canadian thought nothing of venturing into the unknown in a flimsy canoe, living off the land on the way. What impressed newly arrived Frenchmen none too favorably was the Canadians' free and easy ways and their lack of respect for authority. This is not to say that there was no class system, in the colony. Members of *seigneurial* families like the Le Moynes enjoyed a certain social prestige as well as giving the colony its best officers.

As soon as it became obvious that these officers were far more effective in wilderness warfare than the French, the government encouraged young men of good family to enter the army. This they gladly did, for an officer was admired and respected. The procedure went something like this: a father or older brother took a youth in his mid-teens, or even younger, on a campaign as an aide or cadet. When the boy had gained enough experience on the job, the governor might put him in charge of a small war party of his own. Then if he wished to remain in the regular army he might become a lieutenant, or a captain, or a commander of a military post. The Le Moyne brothers followed this pattern. While he was still a child, Bienville saw one brother after another don his uniform and follow Longueuil, or Sérigny, or Iberville to war. In a few short years, death was horribly familiar to him. His brother Saint-Hélène, the best marksman in the colony, was mortally wounded in 1690 defending Quebec against an English colonial army headed by Sir William Phipps. The following year, the whole colony mourned the death of the first Bienville, killed while pursuing an Iroquoian war party which had been ravaging the region around Montreal. Two years later, 18-year-old Chateauguay, who was said to be "able to manage a ship by himself" was killed while taking part in Iberville's expedition against the English at Hudson Bay.

Bienville became a navy cadet at the age of twelve, and he saw his first combat as Iberville's aide in a campaign to expel English fishermen from their villages on the eastern coast of Newfoundland. It was a gruelling initiation for the sixteen-year-old youth. Leaving Placentia, the French settlement on the western shore of the island, on November 1, 1696, Iberville and his party of about 100 men set out due east for Ferryland, sometimes trudging through woods and marshes, sometimes wading up to their waists through ice-cold rivers and streams. By the time they reached Ferryland, their provisions had run out, but they were lucky enough to find a dozen horses which they killed and ate. As they marched northward, conditions grew worse. Their baggage strapped to their backs, they plodded through deep snow, until they were forced to stop and make snowshoes. More than once, a man missed his step and was almost buried in the snow; at other times sharp ice cut through the snowshoes. Nevertheless, the campaign was successful—if one may call the destruction and looting of fishing villages a success—as, one by one, all the settlements except Carbonnear and Bonavists fell to the French. As far as is known, it was on this campaign that Bienville played his first, albeit small, leadership role. He and two other officers led a small contingent across Trinity Bay to Random Sound, captured the settlements, and took forty prisoners.

Before Iberville could consolidate his conquest, he was ordered to set out for Hudson Bay with a fleet of five ships to recapture Port Nelson from the English. Toughened from his Newfoundland experience, Bienville accompanied his brother in the lead ship, the *Pelican*. An older brother, Sérigny, captained the *Profond*. The ships weighed anchor early in July. Sixteen days later they were dodging the ice-filled waters of Hudson Strait. As they edged their path through the ice floes, northern gales knifing through the air, the vessels were separated by dense fog, the *Pelican* in the lead. On September 5, the *Pelican* arrived in front of Port Nelson. A day went by without a sign of the other ships. At dawn the following day, three ships hove into view, but on closer inspection the vessels turned out to be English, not French. Caught between the fort and the three vessels, Iberville had to fight or surrender. He decided to do battle. Batteries were manned and the men took their stations, Bienville and another officer commanding the exposed upper deck. After a series of brilliant maneuvers that culminated in the sinking of one English ship and the capture of another, the English were routed from Port Nelson. In the engagement, Bienville received a wound which would plague him off and on for the rest of his life.

Leaving Sérigny in charge of Port Nelson, Iberville sailed to France, taking Bienville with him. This would be the last time either of the brothers would see Canada again. To prevent a pre-emptive strike by the English, King Louis XIV had decided to establish a post on the banks of the Mississippi River on the land claimed for France by explorer René-Robert Cavelier de La Salle in 1682. In fact, the English promoter Daniel Coxe was already preparing for just such an expedition. Spain was also making plans to thwart France by getting to the mouth of the Mississippi first. It was time for the French to get on the move, and Iberville was the ideal man to lead the venture. In true Le Moyne tradition, Iberville chose a brother to accompany him. At the age of eighteen, Bienville had met his destiny.

Chapter II
A Colony Is Founded

On October 24, 1698, a flotilla sailed out of Brest harbor bound for the Mississippi. The first ship, the *Badine*, was commanded by Iberville with Bienville as one of the officers. The chaplain was the Recollet priest, Father Anastase Douay, who knew something about the river and the native people from his part in La Salle's second expedition. Besides the regular crew, there was also a sprinkling of Canadians, the kind of men who could turn a hand to anything, as long as it did not involve monotonous labor on the land. Following the lead ship was the *Marin* commanded by the Chevalier de Surgères, accompanied by Ensign Sauvolle, who was to play a part in the early history of Louisiana. Two small coastal vessels, or *traversiers*, brought up the rear.

Stored in the hold was the usual assortment of kettles, muskets, hatchets, blankets, and other odds and ends that would appeal to the native people. Besides the provisions for the venture, space was found for pigs, cows, a bull, even a few clucking hens. In his sea chest, Iberville had the "relations"[1] about the Mississippi, written by La Salle's companions, in particular the journals of Father Zénobe Membré who had accompanied the explorer on his first expedition to the mouth of the Mississippi and on his failed sea-search for the elusive delta a few years later.

In less than six weeks the flotilla arrived at Cap Français on the northern coast of Saint Domingue, where it put in for repairs and provisions. There, rumor had it that three English vessels had been spotted in the vicinity. Fearful that the English would grab the prize ahead of him, Iberville set sail with all possible haste for the Gulf of Mexico.

On sighting the coast of Florida, the flotilla cruised cautiously along the shore, on the lookout for a suitable harbor. Late in the evening of January 26, Pensacola Bay loomed before them in the fog. They had found their harbor, and a good one it was, but unfortunately three ships rode at anchor by the shore. Could these be the English ships of the earlier report?

Next morning when the fog lifted, Lieutenant Lescalette was sent ashore for wood and water and, of course, to scout out the lay of the land. Bienville went along as well, disguised as an ordinary seaman, to keep his own eyes and ears open and to prevent the sailors from disclosing the real object of the expedition, which was ostensibly conducting a search for escaped prisoners.

On their arrival at the fort, Lascalette and Bienville played their assigned parts. It transpired that the vessels were not English, but Spanish.

[1]Narrative accounts.

Spain's spy network had known for some time that King Louis XIV hankered after a foothold on the Gulf of Mexico. In order to protect the entrance to the gulf, the viceroy of New Spain was ordered to send a garrison to Pensacola Bay before it fell into the hands of the French, who could use the position to attack Spanish galleons. In fact, the Spaniards had barely arrived before Iberville's fleet showed up. So the Spanish commander, Don Andrés de la Riola, knew full well that Lascalette's talk about escaped prisoners was a fabrication. Masking his feelings with an elaborate display of courtesy, he provided the French with wood and water, and even with a pilot to guide them on their way.

Proceeding westwards, on the alert for any sight of La Salle's harbor, the fleet shortly reached Mobile Point at the entrance to Mobile Bay. The harbor was obviously not the mouth of the mighty Mississippi, but it might provide anchorage for the ships. While they were sounding the channel, the men had their first taste of bad weather. For three days, they were marooned on a little island, which Iberville named Massacre Island, from the heap of skeletons found there. This same island, subsequently named Dauphin Island, was to play a large part in the history of the colony. But that was in the future. For the present, the water was too shallow to permit the vessels to moor on its leeward side.

Continuing on their way, the ships maneuvered their way through the maze of islands which shelter Mississippi Sound. A sudden storm from the south turned the next few days into a sailor's nightmare. On the morning of February 6, Bienville and Lescalette went out to sound the water on the west side of Horn Island (shown on the early maps as Île Bienville) to search for a channel deep enough for the ships to pass to the sheltered northern side, but no channel was to be found. The following day the search continued. Finally, at eight in the evening, Bienville returned with the news that a safe anchorage had been found in the lee of Ship Island, and the following morning the fleet was resting safe and sound in a sheltered harbor.

The worst was over for the time being: the fleet was secure, and according to Iberville's calculations, they were within striking distance of the Mississippi. Seeing smoke on the mainland, he decided to cross over and meet the native inhabitants of the new country and perhaps glean some information about the entrance to the river. He and a few companions set out for the shore in a longboat, with Bienville and two Canadians following in a canoe.

On reaching land, the French could see Indian tracks, but no Indians. After camping for the night, they left a few axes and other odds and ends on the site as a gesture of friendship; then they set out on the trail of the Indians. A few miles onward on the shore of a small bay, Iberville caught a glimpse of the band, but as soon as they saw him they fled into the forest, leaving a sick old man behind them. Iberville treated the old man kindly, fed him, gave him a smoke, and placed him by a warm fire. Meanwhile Bienville accompanied by two companions had set off in a canoe to search for the other natives. That evening he came upon an old woman and took her back to the French camp, where she was also well treated. The next day several companions cautiously approached, and the following day a few more. As a token of friendship, the peace pipe was passed around and each side prepared a feast for the other. Leaving Bienville and two Canadians on the shore as hostages, Iberville invited three of the braves on board the French ship, where the guns were fired for their edification.

The sound of the guns brought in some members of the Bayogoula and the Mugulasha tribes who happened to be hunting nearby. The newcomers were also treated royally and presented with a few gifts. At a feast of sagamite[2] and prunes, Iberville presented the chief with a massive peace pipe shaped like a ship to cement the friendship between the French and all the local tribes. On their side, the Bayogoulas promised to return to the same place in four days' time when their hunt was over to feast the French and guide them to the great river. Much to Iberville's disappointment, the rendezvous was not kept, so the faithful Bienville was sent off to look for them. All he managed to find were two women who informed him that the Bayogoulas had returned to the Mississippi in search of food.

It was time to prepare for the final leg of the journey. Back at Ship Island, two *traversiers* were fitted out, each carrying twenty men and provisions for twenty days. Iberville and Bienville commanded the lead boat, followed by Ensign Sauvolle and Father Douay. Captain Surgères and the rest of the crew stayed at Ship Island with the remaining vessels.

The expedition set out on February 27. For several days the light craft pushed through driving headwinds laced with torrential rain. Iberville was about to run his boat aground to avoid being swamped by the waves when he spotted a ribbon of water between two towering rocks and steered towards it. By great good luck, he had found the North Pass of the Mississippi River.

Inching his way between the rocks, which turned out to be petrified trees borne down by the current, he tasted the water. It was fresh. The white, swirling current, so different from the blue waters of the gulf, was exactly as La Salle had described it. In their hearts the men were convinced that the river stretching before them was the Mississippi, but Iberville had to have better proof to silence possible doubters in France.

[2]A thin gruel of husked corn mixed with fish, berries, and other edibles that might be available.

Next morning, Shrove Tuesday, Father Douay said mass and the men joined in a jubilant *Te Deum* in thanksgiving for the discovery. Afterwards, the boats continued up the deepening river, Bienville scouting ahead in a birchbark canoe. Every morning the camping places were marked with a cross, and every evening the guns boomed out to attract the attention of the Indians, yet no Indians appeared. After five days of hard rowing against the current, they spotted six canoes. At the sight of the two large boats, the natives made for the shore and disappeared, except for one courageous fellow who held his ground. The man succeeded in inducing his companions to join him, and soon the natives were happily trading dried meat for French knives and axes. One of their number was also persuaded to board Bienville's canoe and guide the party to the Bayogoula village.

On March 14 they reached the village, which the Bayogoulas shared with the Mugulashas. Bearing aloft a large calumet[3] adorned with multicolored feathers, an old battle-scarred chief accompanied by three braves paddled out to welcome the newcomers. At the village a pleasant surprise awaited the French: one of the chiefs was dressed in a blue French army coat. Obviously a Frenchman had passed that way before. Bienville, who had already picked up a smattering of the local dialect from his guide, was able to make out the fact that La Salle's companion, Henry de Tonty, had passed through the village on his way up and down the river. Asked about a fork in the river, the chief replied that no fork existed. This did not square with the "relations," all of which mentioned a fork. Iberville was perplexed. All his own observations suggested that they had found the Mississippi; still the niggling doubt remained. To make assurance doubly sure, he determined to push on to the Houma village, although he was impatient to return to the ships. Already he was ninety leagues from the harbor, and he had told Surgères to return to France without him if he was not back in six weeks.

After another day of ceremonial feasting with their friendly hosts, the party set out again, escorted by several Bayogoulas. For four more days the men continued their laborious journey against the swift current, all the while cursing the false accounts which made the journey necessary. A few miles north of Baton Rouge, they reached the landing place leading to the Houma village, where the French were welcomed with the usual round of ceremonies, followed by singing and dancing. The Houmas also talked about Tonty who had spent five days in their village, and they too insisted that the river had no fork. Nonetheless, Iberville decided that the expedition would have to push on to the village of the Koroas. On March 22, they set out with six Houmas and one Tensas to guide the party along. That

[3]A pipe used to burn tobacco as an offering to the Great Spirit and as a sign of friendship.

evening Iberville took the Tensas aside, grilled him about the Indian tribes and had him draw a map of the Mississippi. The result was the same: the drawing showed no forks. Surely all the Indians could not be making the same mistake? The matter was clinched for good when a Bayogoula chief announced that Tonty had left a letter with the chief of the Mugulashas "to give to a man who would come from the sea." Iberville surmised correctly that the letter had been intended for La Salle, who had been expected to reach the Mississippi Delta in 1686. There could be no further doubt about it; the documents were wrong. The river was undoubtedly the Mississippi. It was time to return to the coast and build a fort.

Floating swiftly with the current, the party reached Bayou Manchac the following afternoon. Accompanied by a Mugulasha guide, Iberville took a short cut from there to the coast by way of Lake Pontchartrain and Lake Maurepas, both lakes named after Jérôme Phélypeaux de Maurepas, Comte de Pontchartrain, the man in charge of the colonies. Bienville and Sauvolle continued down the Mississippi with the main party, stopping off at the Bayogoula village to buy corn.

Bienville's party ran into trouble at the village because of the insensitivity of Father Douay. Having mislaid his breviary and his journal, the priest kept insisting that the village be searched until the books were found. His weeping and complaining, and the not too subtle implication that he had been robbed by the Indians, so insulted the chief that he refused to supply the party with grain. Fortunately, the books turned up and tempers cooled down. In the search, Bienville also discovered Tonty's all-important letter. At last the French had written proof that the river they had found was the Mississippi.

By noon on March 31 Iberville was back on board the *Badine*, where he was joined a few hours later by Bienville and the rest of the contingent. The next item of business was to find a place for a settlement, and to find it soon before provisions ran low. With Bienville's help, Iberville explored the coast for a spot which could be easily defended and at the same time block the entrance to the Mississippi. After much futile searching, they chose a location on the eastern shore of Biloxi Bay, near present-day Ocean Springs, Mississippi. Never meant to be a permanent settlement, it was the best Iberville could do in the time at his disposal. In making the choice, he reasoned that it was strategically placed, sheltered from the winds, and close to three friendly Indian tribes—the Biloxi, the Pascagoulas, and the Moctoby. Finally, nearby Ship Island would afford safe anchorage for sea-going vessels.

Work on the fort went ahead quickly enough, despite the rainy weather and the difficulty in felling trees thick enough to break the axes. Boats shuttled from ship to shore carrying food, building materials, artillery, and animals. All through the month of April, the sound of saw and hammer resounded in the wilderness as the fort began to take shape. Fort Maurepas, as it was named, was constructed of logs laid one on another and protected by four bastions and a stout palisade.

The fort completed, Iberville prepared for his departure. Ensign Sauvolle was left in charge, with Bienville as second in command. The garrison of about eighty consisted of several Canadians, thirteen "gentle" (!) buccaneers that Iberville had engaged at Cap Français, and a complement of soldiers, sailors, and workmen. Finally, on May 1, the *Badine* and the *Marin* hoisted sails for the voyage to France.

After Iberville's departure work continued on the fort. Trees were felled, ground cleared, and seedlings planted in the open spaces. Once they had completed their lodgings, the men were put to work building a warehouse, a chapel, and a makeshift hospital, which unfortunately was to see more use than they had bargained for. As spring passed into summer, the sun beat mercilessly down on the hot sand, making life at the settlement almost unbearable. Freshly sown crops, which had initially shown great promise, began to wither and die on the vine, snakes and alligators crept up to the very gates of the fort, and borers ate away at the keels of the boats. To make matters worse, the supply of fresh water dwindled to a trickle, and if a spring had not eventually been found a few miles from the fort, the men would surely have been laid low with fever. As it was, several of them did become weak and ill. With lethargy came depression and indiscipline. Cooped up in their little pocket fort, day in day out, the motley group of sailors, soldiers, Canadians, and buccaneers made a habit of hoarding their ration of brandy and then going on a drunken binge.

By all accounts, Bienville kept his spirits up. Of course the young man was away from the fort a good part of the time exploring the country and visiting the native tribes. Some of these expeditions could have cost him his life. Towards the end of May he set out with a party of ten men and a visiting Bayogoula chief as escort for the land of the Colapissas, a small nation living north of Lake Pontchartrain. When they sighted the Colapissa village, they found the Colapissas armed and ready for battle. It must have been a tense moment for the little party: one false move could bring a lethal hail of arrows in their direction. At the very least, a confrontation could scuttle any hopes of a peace treaty with the Colapissas, and probably with their allies as well, the very thing that Bienville wished to avoid, for he knew the value of Indian friendship and the terror of their wars. To defuse the issue, the French fell back and Bienville dispatched the Bayogoula chief to find out what the hostile display was all about. It transpired that it was a case of mistaken identity. A few days earlier, the village had been the victim of a slave-raiding attack by the Chickasaws led by two English traders from Carolina, and the ten Frenchmen were taken for English. On learning that the newcomers were actually enemies of the English and opposed to slave trading, the Colapissas laid down their arms. After the usual courtesies and exchange of gifts, Bienville cemented an alliance with yet another nation.

Early in June, he set out on another exploring expedition. Seeing that deltas and shifting sands prevented large vessels from sailing up the Mississippi by way of the North Pass, it was imperative to find another anchorage, if one existed. Ship Island was all very well, but it was not on the mainland; besides, it was becoming more and more obvious that Biloxi was a poor place for a settlement. If only the Spaniards would leave—and there were rumors to that effect from Spanish deserters—Pensacola would be ideal. On his travels, Bienville circled the coast, sounding the harbors and rivers as far as Mobile. Everywhere he went, he and his men were received with great cordiality, but they found no suitable harbor. From Mobile they made their way by land within sight of Pensacola. Alas, the Spaniards were still there, and enlarging their fort.

Shortly after his return to Biloxi there was a little excitement at Fort Maurepas. Father Davion and Father Montigny, two priests from the Quebec seminary, a branch of the Seminary of the Foreign Missions in France, accompanied by a dozen Canadians and a few native people appeared out of the blue for a visit. Word of Iberville's arrival in Louisiana had reached the priests in their missions on the Upper Mississippi, so they came down to find out all they could about the venture. If the king decided to found a permanent settlement on the lower river, the priests hoped that they, not the Jesuits, would be placed in charge of the missions to the Indians, as indeed they ultimately were. This decision was to have far-reaching consequences for Bienville and for the church in Louisiana.

In late August, Bienville was on his travels again. Accompanied by five men, he explored the area around Lake Pontchartrain and Lake Maurepas and the navigable bayous nearby. After crossing the lakes, he came to a little stream which he named Bayou St. Jean in honor of his patron saint. Leading from Lake Pontchartrain to the Mississippi River, the bayou made an excellent shortcut from the river to the Bay of Biloxi. On a visit to the Bayogoulas, he found those natives agitated because of a surprise attack made on them by the Houmas. In his role of peacemaker and guarantor of peace, he dissuaded the Bayogoulas from making a retaliatory attack, assuring his hosts that the French would see that the Houmas made amends. Following the visit, as he was rounding a bend in the Mississippi, known afterwards as English Turn, a twelve-gun corvette hove into view. It was an English vessel, the *Carolina Galley*, commanded by one Captain Bond whom Iberville and he had earlier encountered in Hudson Bay. With considerable aplomb, the twenty-year-old Bienville in his little birch bark canoe ordered Bond to leave the river or else be forced to leave, since France had prior claims to the Mississippi. Not so, said Bond; the English had a better right to the river than the French. All the same, Bond turned his corvette around and left. As a parting shot, he warned Bienville that the English would be back in force the following year.

As it happened, Captain Bond was employed by the same Daniel Coxe who had been hoping to beat Iberville to the Mississippi. Coxe had fitted out an expedition—ironically consisting of Huguenots fleeing from religious persecution in France—and sailed to Carolina just when the French were setting out for Louisiana. After wintering in Carolina, Bond went ahead, discovered the mouth of the river, and sailed upstream until he had the bad luck to run into Bienville. Apparently Bienville had a chance to speak to the Huguenot refugees, who begged him to petition King Louis XIV to allow them to settle in Louisiana and practice their religion in peace. Nothing came of the request; for no monarch of the day, Catholic or Protestant, could believe that people who professed a religion other than the king's could be a loyal subject. As events proved, Louisiana's loss was Carolina's gain. From their first arrival in the English colony, the Huguenots were highly regarded for their thrifty and law-abiding ways. Instead of sallying forth into the wilderness in search of profit and adventure as the French were prone to do, they rooted themselves firmly in their new homeland and developed prosperous farms and businesses, whereas Louisiana was always short of hardy peasants.

Back in Biloxi, the days dragged wretchedly by. Then on January 8, 1700, cannon booms announced the return of Iberville and Surgères. Together with welcome supplies and provisions, Iberville brought along two commissions from the king: the first for Sauvolle as commandant, and the second for Bienville as king's lieutenant, the man who would officially replace Sauvolle in an emergency.

Among the new arrivals were several interesting characters. For the spiritual health of French and Indian alike, there was the young Jesuit priest Father Du Ru. Also along was a carpenter and man-of-all-trades named André Pénigaut, whose memoirs were to make him famous. Among the officers on board was a clutch of Canadians closely associated with the history of Louisiana: Chateauguay,[4] the youngest Le Moyne brother; Louis Juchereau de Saint Denis, a relative of Iberville's wife; and Pierre Dugué de Boisbriant, a Le Moyne cousin and former companion in arms. Another Le Moyne relative, Pierre Charles Le Sueur, came out to explore for copper

[4]Antoine de Chateauguay, who had received the title of his dead brother Louis de Chateauguay.

mines in the Upper Mississippi Valley. In reality, the discovery of mines wherever they might be found, was the navy minister's top priority. With all the mineral deposits that had been found in Mexico, Pontchartrain reasoned that there had to be rich seams in Louisiana. To help search for the metals, Sérigny, another Le Moyne brother, had recruited sixty Canadians who would act as scouts and guides for La Sueur. And when the mines were discovered, as the minister confidently expected, Iberville was authorized to hire native people to work them—and pay them—a fairly novel approach for the time.

Bienville's story of his encounter with Captain Bond confirmed Iberville's suspicions about "the restless English" and their expansionist designs. Before mining or exploring, the entrance to the Mississippi had to be protected. In February, Bienville, accompanied by a Bayogoula guide, went searching for a spot which would not be submerged at high water. About thirty miles below the present New Orleans, on the eastern side of the river the guide pointed out a wooded bluff, which always remained dry, or so he said. Iberville drew up plans for the new fort, christened Fort de la Boulaye but more commonly known as Fort Mississippi, a crude little affair providing no more than a token defense of the river. When Father Gravier saw it the following year, he was not overly impressed: "There is neither fort nor bastion, nor entrenchments, nor redoubts," he said; "it consists of only a battery of six pieces of cannon placed on the edge of a hill; and five or six cabins detached from one another and roofed with palm leaves."[5] Contrary to the Bayogoula chief's assurance, the ground was often flooded and mired in mud. Even worse, there was no fresh water nearby, and the men in the garrison were constantly ridden by fever. But while it was there, the crude outpost served as a lookout point until a more solid fort could be constructed.

The hammering and sawing were going on apace when Henry de Tonty arrived, accompanied by twenty Canadian traders. "Great salvos, great clamor, great joy," says Father Du Ru. Tonty was an old friend of Iberville and a major explorer in his own right, respected by the native people for his endurance and courage. As previously stated, he had been up and down the Mississippi, once with La Salle, and once more in search of La Salle who was supposed to be setting up a colony at the mouth of the river. What he did not know at the time was that the unfortunate explorer had overshot the delta and had already met his end in the Texas wilderness at the hands of his own men. Upon discovering the truth, Tonty set out to look for the explorer's abandoned colony which was known to be located near Matagorda

[5]Reuben G. Thwaites, ed. *The Jesuit Relations and Allied Documents*, 65 (Cleveland, 1896-1901), 121. Hereinafter cited *Jesuit Relations*.

Bay, Texas. Half starved and abandoned by his companions, he was forced to turn back after penetrating as far as the present Houston County. All things considered, Tonty was just the man to guide Iberville on a projected expedition up the Red River as far as the great village of the Cenis Indians, the site of La Salle's colony and a stepping stone towards the fabled mines of Spanish America.

However, there was a hitch in the plan. Iberville was struck down with such violent pain in his knees (probably rheumatism or arthritis) that he was unable to walk, making a trek into the wilderness out of the question. Besides, Tonty's services were required for a peace-making mission. Apparently at the instigation of English slave traders, the Chickasaws, the most warlike of all the Mississippi tribes, were repeatedly making forays against the Choctaws and other neighboring tribes in order to capture slaves. Anxious to put an end to the strife, Iberville dispatched Tonty to Chickasaw country, in what is now the northern section of Mississippi, to negotiate a treaty between the Chickasaws and their native foes and to persuade them to banish the English from their villages. In his stead, Bienville was chosen to lead the important expedition to the Cenis.

On March 22, 1700, Bienville set off on his journey of exploration, accompanied by Juchereau de St. Denis, twenty Canadians, six Tensas guides, and one Wichita who claimed to have visited the Spanish settlements. The journey through the marshes and swamps of what is now northern Louisiana was not one for a tenderfoot. Before the week was out Bienville had two sick men on his hands; and the Tensas guides, tired of slogging through oozing mud, refused to go any farther.

That spring seems to have been exceptionally cold and wet. Day after day the men were forced to hack their way through canebrakes, or wade through icy streams up to their waists and even higher. As Bienville naively wrote in his journal, a medium-sized man like himself was always at a disadvantage in deep water. Whereas his taller companions could wade through comfortably enough, he reported, he and others like him were almost submerged as they struggled along, pushing their packages ahead of them on planks. When the streams were too deep to ford, the men fashioned crude rafts or swam across, after discharging their guns to scare off the alligators. The nights were the worst. More often than not, the men had to lie down in their damp clothes on logs laid side by side to raise them above the mud and water. On good days they shot turkeys, deer, even the odd buffalo that roamed on prairies interspersed between the seemingly endless swamps; at other times, they had to go to bed hungry. Yet, no matter how low they felt, Bienville tells us, they made a point of singing and joking, to show their guides that they were better men than the Spaniards!

Along the way, they made contact with several tribes clustered by the banks of the Red River: the Wichita, the Natchitoches, the Souchoninos, and the Nakasis, all of whom were friendly and hospitable enough as far as their poor means would allow. The last tribe they visited was the Yatasis. Apparently the natives had advance word of their arrival, so they hid their pirogues and their Indian corn, suspecting correctly that their visitors would want to buy them. But Bienville was not a Le Moyne for nothing. He told the chief that if he could not buy the corn and the boats he and his men would be obliged to stay at the village for a while. The prospect of feeding twenty hungry men was enough to make the chief change his mind.

The following day the group set off for the Cadodaquois country, but the guides gave such varying accounts about the distance and location that Bienville decided to fall back. Many of the men were ill from the cold and bad food; besides, the time limit given to him by Iberville was fast approaching and he was afraid of delaying his brother's departure for France. Although he had failed to reach his goal, the expedition was by no means a failure. Even if he had not located the mines, he had pushed his way across the entire breadth of Louisiana and learned a great deal about the land and the people. Some Cadodaquois natives whom he encountered also told him that the Spaniards often came on horseback to their country for Indian corn. Using a few coins as illustration, Bienville questioned the natives about Spanish mines. They had never seen the Spaniards dig ore out of the ground, they told him, although they had seen them use such objects when playing cards, and they stamped their feet and tore up the cards when they lost. The diary ends there. The remainder was indecipherable since it was completely sodden, Iberville later told the minister.

On May 18, Bienville reached Biloxi, where he found his brother making final preparations for departure. Ten days later, Iberville set sail for France, leaving Sauvolle in charge of Fort Maurepas and Bienville to oversee the new fort on the Mississippi.

For the next several months, Bienville lived at the new fort by the river. How he occupied himself is not recorded—very likely he continued exploring the land and making contact with the native people. When Father Gravier visited Fort Mississippi in December 1700, he painted a gloomy picture of the place:

> This post is on the South side of the river, 18 leagues from its mouth; . . . The Commandant, Monsieur de Bienville, has a very small and very neat house. I observed on arriving that the men were commencing to suffer from hunger, and that the flour was beginning to fail. . . . If the Mississippi country be settled, the fort will be transported to . . . the Bayogoulas . . . for the high waters flood the place to such an extent that the men spent four months in the water; and frequently had to wade mid-leg deep in it outside their cabins. . . .

> The wheat that had been sown was already quite high, when the inundation caused by a heavy sea in the month of August, carried it away. The garden did not succeed any better; and besides there are a great number of black snakes that eat the lettuce and other vegetables down to the roots.[6]

Meanwhile the situation at Biloxi was deteriorating by the day. Supplies of flour and bacon were perilously low and the wine had almost run out. Without the Indian corn supplied by the neighboring tribes, the plight of the garrison would have been desperate indeed. By summer when there was little or no hunting, a few of the precious cattle transported all the way from France had to be slaughtered to feed the sick. To compound the problem, far too many people came to Biloxi to await Iberville's return, and all of them had to be fed. Tonty put in an appearance with two missionaries, Father Limoges and Father Montigny; and Le Sueur and his men were back from Sioux country with a cargo of blue earth, which unhappily turned out to be worthless clay. All these, together with a stray *voyageur*[7] here and there and a sprinkling of native visitors drained the resources to the limit. As the months rolled by without any sign of Iberville, Sauvolle became disheartened with everything and everybody. According to his account, the Indians were friendly and hospitable enough, but they were a sorry lot; and the country was hardly worth keeping unless mines were to be found. The hot climate and poor rations were devastating the garrison, particularly the Canadians, many of whom were either sick, or unruly, or both. Even the Jesuit priest, Father Du Ru came in for his share of criticism for impertinence. Very likely Sauvolle himself was in the throes of illness when he penned his report, for he died two weeks later.

After Sauvolle's death, Bienville left Fort Mississippi to take command at Biloxi. One can imagine the gloom that descended on the inhabitants of Fort Maurepas as they waited in vain for Iberville's arrival. For three months the soldiers in the garrison were reduced to a diet of Indian corn, which they detested, and even that was scarce. Lethargy gave way to despair as more and more men sickened and died. In a matter of months several bodies were interred in the little churchyard.

Unknown to Bienville, Iberville had been laid low with malaria for several weeks after his return to France. Upon his recovery, more time was taken up debating future plans for the Mississippi colony. Iberville proposed to the minister that the French should remove themselves from

[6] *Jesuit Relations*, 65:161-3.

[7] A man who spent his time transporting furs or other goods to and from remote stations.

Biloxi and establish a post on Mobile Bay to keep the English in check and strengthen the relations with the nearby tribes, especially the powerful Choctaws, whose hunting grounds extended over a large area of Mississippi between 32 and 33 degrees North Latitude. With the new post and a strengthened fort on the Mississippi River, the colony would be sealed against foreign invasion. The next step would be to persuade the Spaniards to give up Pensacola—which was not such a far-fetched idea as might appear on the surface. That same year King Louis XIV's grandson had ascended the Spanish throne, so there was reason to believe that the sovereigns of France and Spain would be united in policy as they were in blood. Iberville argued that it would actually be in Spain's best interest to leave, since Pensacola was a useless post without settlers or substantial Indian allies, just begging to be captured by the English. On the other hand, if Spain abandoned its dog-in-the-manger policy, a strong Franco-Spanish alliance could keep their mutual enemy out of other Spanish possessions in North America—and not incidentally, of course, out of the Mississippi Valley as well. Iberville's proposal only served to antagonize the Spanish junta; to their way of thinking, the French themselves were interlopers on territory granted to Spain by Pope Alexander VI back in 1493.

The political maneuvering was still in progress when Iberville departed on his third and final voyage to Louisiana. Two more Le Moyne brothers took part in the expedition—the experienced naval officer, Joseph de Sérigny; and twenty-year-old Gabriel D'Assigny, the only Le Moyne who was not in the military. (The latter remained in Cap Français to serve as a counsellor and he died there a few months later.) Also aboard to act as commissary for the new colony was Nicolas de La Salle—no relation to the great La Salle, although he had been with the explorer on his voyage to the Mississippi. He was the first man to uproot his wife and children for what he hoped would be a better life in Louisiana.

During a stopover at Cap Français, Iberville refitted his vessels and took on some horses, cattle, and pigs for the colony. He also dispatched a supply boat ahead to Biloxi, together with orders to evacuate Fort Maurepas and transport everything to the site to be known as Mobile. Meanwhile, he himself put in at Pensacola to inform the acting governor, Don Francisco Martinez, about the proposed new post. The ensuing diplomatic *pas de deux* was not without its share of comedy, Martinez protesting in elaborately polite terms that the Mobile area was a Spanish possession, and Iberville equally politely insisting that he had to obey his king's orders. Yet when Martinez asked for the loan of a French ship in order to send a messenger to Vera Cruz for supplies and for instructions from the viceroy about how to handle the situation, Iberville was happy to oblige; and the governor lent Iberville a ketch to transport French workmen to the new post.

A recurrence of his old illness kept Iberville on board ship until the middle of February. From his sick bed, he sent word to Bienville to betake himself to Dauphin Island, where he would be joined by Chateauguay, Sérigny, and several workmen. The next few weeks were scenes of much activity at Dauphin Island and Mobile. Under Bienville's direction, the men set to work building a storehouse on the eastern side of the island where there was a good harbor. Once the building was under way, Chateauguay and La Salle were left to supervise its completion; and Bienville with Sérigny and Lieutenant Charles Le Vasseur sailed up the Mobile River to a point "sixteen leagues off at the second bluff." There on a wooded spot raised more than twenty feet above the water, work commenced on the new post to be named Fort Louis.

According to contemporary accounts, the fort was made of logs laid "piece on piece," sixty *toises* [about 384 feet] square, reinforced with four bastions, each having a battery of six guns. Inside the fort was the parade ground, surrounded by four groups of buildings—the chapel, the storehouse, the officers' quarters and the guardhouse. Barracks for the soldiers and the Canadians were to be built outside the fort on the west bank of the Mobile River.

As soon as Iberville's health improved, he sailed to Fort Louis and drew up plans for the streets of the town which was expected to develop west and north of the fort. It was laid out in block formation large enough to allow each inhabitant to have a plot of land for a garden. Bienville had a substantial plot close to the fort, with similar plots for Tonty, La Salle, Le Sueur, and Boisbriant. Plots were also reserved for the Jesuits and the Foreign Missions priests.

Iberville's last job was to make peace with the Chickasaws, the nation that could pose the greatest threat to the new colony. In March, Tonty returned from his mission to that nation accompanied by several Choctaw and Chickasaw chiefs who wished to hear what the French leader had to say. On their arrival, Iberville presented the chiefs with rifles, powder, kettles, knives, awls, and other gifts for their tribes. The next day with Bienville as interpreter, he made his formal speech. He rebuked the Chickasaws for their slave-driven attacks on the Choctaws in which so many lives had been lost on both sides. Warming to his theme, he harangued them about their so-called friends, the Carolinians, whose ultimate purpose, he declared, was to weaken and enslave all the Indians and then grab their lands for themselves. After this dire prediction, he told them they would have to expel the English from their villages and stop warring with their neighbors, or else he would arm all the tribes against them. However, he went on, if the Chickasaws were willing to cooperate, he would establish a trading post in their territory where they would get all the trade goods they needed at a good price. As evidence of his good intentions, he offered to send a young French boy named Petit Michel to live with them and learn their language; and he sweetened the pot with extra presents for all the chiefs themselves. Whatever they thought about his bluster, the Chickasaws were impressed with Iberville's generosity. Where their own self-interest was concerned, one white man was probably as welcome as another. If they could be assured of getting a good supply of guns, blankets, and hatchets, their allegiance might be assured. At all events, they enthusiastically agreed to come to terms with the neighboring tribes, and Iberville gave them an escort to lead them safely home.

Before leaving for France, Iberville wrote to all the missionaries advising them of the new *Pax Gallica* and asking them to use their influence to promote the peace in their own mission fields. He also wrote to Father Bergier, the vicar of the bishop of Quebec, requesting missionaries for the Chickasaws and the Choctaws. As he knew from his experience in Canada, the missionary was as much a diplomat as he was a man of the cloth.

Well pleased with his progress, he sailed for France on March 31, leaving Bienville in charge until he himself would return the following year. To be sure, there was still much to be done to consolidate the shaky new alliance with the Indians and to encourage the migration of good solid French citizens who would settle down in the new colony, till the land, and raise families. Little did he know that he would never see Louisiana again. A projected voyage in 1703 had to be postponed because of his illness. When he rallied, his services were required in the War of the Spanish Succession, which pitted France and Spain against a large European coalition. Commanding a fleet of twelve ships, he and his brother Sérigny were sent to harass the English in the West Indies. Before the campaign was over, he was stricken with yellow fever and he died in Havana. So it was that at the age of twenty-two, Bienville was about to take control of the new colony for a long time to come.

Chapter III
Bienville's First Administration

It was just as well for Bienville's peace of mind that he could not foresee what lay ahead when he bade farewell to his older brother. As far as he knew at the time, Louisiana's future looked quite hopeful. The initial groundwork had been laid, and Iberville was expected back the following year with provisions and settlers. The establishment at Mobile was a far cry from the plague-ridden quarters at Biloxi and the harbor on Dauphin Island was commodious and well sheltered. Exploration of the coastline and waterways was getting off to a good start, with further probes into the interior already in the planning stage. For the time being, the two most powerful nations, the Choctaws and the Chickasaws, were at peace and the smaller nations around Mobile could be counted upon for corn and game.

To be sure there were still problems ahead. To keep the Chickasaws on their side, the French would have to honor Iberville's promise to establish a trading post in the area between the Chickasaw and Choctaw homelands and keep it well stocked with trade goods. This would involve a considerable initial infusion from the royal purse, because French merchants were notoriously slow to risk their own money in fledgling colonies. More royal funds would be needed to help defray the expenses of prospective settlers. In addition, there were several influential naysayers abroad, all proclaiming that the colony would be more trouble than it was worth. Governor Louis-Hector de Callières of Canada and the Quebec fur merchants predicted that Louisiana would be the ruin of Canada if, as they suspected, unlicensed fur traders managed to smuggle their wares down the Mississippi; Governor Jean-Baptiste Ducasse of Saint Domingue disapproved of the venture; and Captain Taneguy Le Gallois de Beaujeu, the naval commander on La Salle's expedition, let it be known that he "feared" Iberville's colony would fare no better than La Salle's. Nonetheless, at the French court, where intrigue was a way of life, Iberville enjoyed the patronage of the navy minister, Jérôme de Pontchartrain, a vigorous partisan of French overseas imperialism. Unfortunately, Iberville's recurring illness after the third voyage delayed assistance to Louisiana at a very critical time, and his death deprived Bienville of an influential voice at court.

The onset of the War of the Spanish Succession in 1702 dealt the colony its worst blow. As the conflict dragged on, France suffered a string of military defeats in Europe and increasing poverty at home. As a result, Louisiana was largely abandoned to its own meagre resources at a time when it was still dependent on the mother country for everything—food, clothing, tools, ammunition, trade goods for the native people, and a thousand and one other items. Inevitably, the demands of the war restricted the number of supply ships to the colony, and the provisions were always too little, too late. Further complicating matters was the appalling inefficiency and confusion—not to say downright corruption—that prevailed everywhere. For example, on his way to Saint Domingue, the Comte de Choiseul had his own furniture placed on board ship while dried vegetables for Louisiana were left lying at the docks. Pilfering was common. Ships' officers and crew members turned a dishonest penny by stashing away and selling some of the provisions so sorely needed in the colony. Bienville had many a horror story to relate: flour and bacon arrived spoiled; soldiers' uniforms, exposed to the elements or shoved in with nails, were unwearable, condemning the soldiers to go about in rags; wine barrels leaked; and the list goes on.

Iberville's own activities in the war came under government scrutiny after his death. In the investigation which followed, it was discovered that almost everyone involved in the West Indian campaign from the Comte de Chavagnac and the Comte de Choiseul, to Iberville and Sérigny, French merchants, and ships' officers, had lined their own pockets in one way or another. The two brothers, and Bienville as well, were also suspected of having defrauded the king in Louisiana by dipping into the stores and using the royal vessels for their own use. Although the accusations against Bienville were never substantiated, they haunted him for years. Consequently, a certain mistrust attended everything he said and did, and many of his requests for the welfare of the colony were rejected out of hand, even while the minister grudgingly admitted that the young man was masterful in his dealings with the Indians.

It would be going too far to use the term "separate but equal" to describe the relationship between any European colony and the native inhabitants; yet, for a white man, Bienville treated the Indians remarkably well. His friends and foes alike, even if they agreed on nothing else, agreed on this. He listened to their complaints and participated in their rituals without any show of the lofty superiority which they had come to expect and which they so resented from Europeans. What especially pleased them was the fact that he did them the courtesy of learning their language, so they could participate with him in the normal give and take of conversation. When they came to Mobile, he entertained them at his own table, and they felt free to enter and leave his house as if they were at home. There is no doubt that he was tough, and he could be devious, but he was fair. If he punished an Indian for an unprovoked attack on a Frenchman, he did not hesitate to punish a Frenchman for a similar offense against a native person. More than anything else, it was probably his adroit handling of Indian matters that saved the colony during its darkest years.

Bienville's ability to deal with the Indians was put to the test soon enough. In April 1702 eight important Alabama chiefs came to Mobile and he persuaded them to make peace with the Chickasaws and the Mobiliens. In themselves, the Alabamans were a small nation numbering about 1,200 souls, but they were a brave and warlike people and their land was strategically located on the Alabama River, which led directly to the powerful Creek tribes. Before the French came to settle at Mobile, the Alabamans had been loyal allies of the Carolinians for over a decade. With the weapons they received from English traders, they terrorized the smaller tribes in search of captives for the lucrative slave market in Charles Town.[1]

Naturally the Carolinians had no intention of sitting idly by and letting their old allies defect to the French. Besides, there was more involved in this frontier competition than slaves or deerskins. Governor James Moore of South Carolina understood very well that the example of the Alabamans could encourage neighboring tribes to desert in a body to the French, leaving the English colonies vulnerable to attack. In his mind, a way had to be found to bring the Alabamans back to the fold and reclaim the river route to the Mississippi Valley. So a few "sensible men" loaded with presents and assurances of future assistance were dispatched to the Alabama villages.

Apparently the ploy worked. In May 1703 two Alabama chiefs came to Mobile with the false report that the English had left the Alabama country. Bienville was completely fooled. At the invitation of the chiefs, he sent a man named Le Brie and four Canadians to buy some corn for the garrison. On the way, the men were ambushed and four killed. The lone survivor managed to swim to safety after sustaining a hatchet blow on the arm.

This unprovoked attack had to be avenged, for unless punishment was exacted, as the system of frontier justice demanded, French prestige would suffer and French lives would be held in contempt. As soon as provisions arrived from France, Bienville began preparations for an expedition against the Alabamans. Since his army would have to travel about 400 miles into unknown territory, he needed guides. The Mobiliens, one-time allies of the Alabamans and familiar with the territory, offered their services. To complement his own small army of about sixty men he invited the Choctaws, the Pascagoulas, the Thomés, and the Mobiliens to join forces with him. Pirogues were constructed, food was prepared for the journey, and guns and ammunition distributed to the principal warriors. When everything was ready, Bienville, Tonty, St. Denis, and sixty men set out for a pre-arranged rendezvous with the natives.

Very soon things began to unravel. Most of Bienville's allies were bow-and-arrow Indians unaccustomed to handling the white man's

[1]Now known as Charleston.

ammunition. Heedless of warnings not to approach the camp fire too closely with the gunpowder, two poor Indians forgot the warning and were so badly burned that they died two days later. In the Indian belief system, this was a bad omen. As if to confirm their gloomy prognostications, several warriors fell ill, leading others to slip away and head for home. Quite reasonably from their point of view, they saw no reason to risk their lives in a white man's expedition, and a doomed one at that. To add to his worries, Bienville did not really trust his Mobilien guides. At a council of war it was decided that the French would conduct the attack on their own. Using the illnesses and defections as an excuse, Bienville made a pretence of retreating and dismissed the Indians. Then he set off with forty-eight men to launch what was intended to be a surprise attack on the Alabamans. After a ten-day journey by land and water they spied the enemy's campfire, and when night came they made their move. As they were sneaking up on the Alabamans through canes and blackberry bushes, a few twigs broke, alerting the Alabamans, all but two of whom managed to escape with their lives. Two Frenchmen were also killed in the encounter.

The whole episode taught Bienville a valuable lesson. A punitive campaign into unknown territory where the enemy could appear and disappear at will was far too risky; it could even be the end of the tiny colony. That is not to say that he abandoned the eye-for-an-eye and tooth-for-a-tooth system of frontier justice. If at all possible, he pressured Indian chiefs to punish members of their own tribes who made unwarranted attacks on the French, or else bring the offenders to Mobile for punishment. When all else failed, he encouraged his Indian allies to attack the aggressors, even if it meant that the punishment was not as swift as he himself might have liked. It took almost two years, for example, before he was able to persuade the Arkansas to avenge the deaths of the French missionary Father Foucault and his three traveling companions who had been beaten to death by their Koroan guides. As for the Alabamans, Bienville encouraged friendly Indians, particularly the Choctaws, to harass them every chance they got and he paid them for scalps and captives.

Meanwhile he had to cope with troubles on another front. Faced with a desperate shortage of trade goods, he found himself unable to supply the needs of the Chickasaws, let alone build the promised fort in their territory. And even if the post had been feasible, he could not spare enough men to guard it. All this played into the hands of the English. The Chickasaws were a nation of hunters rather than farmers, and they needed guns to stalk the deer. More than anything else, it was probably the promise of French arms and gunpowder, which was of better quality than the English variety, that induced the Chickasaws to make an accord with Iberville in the first place. On their visits to Mobile in 1703, the Chickasaws could see for themselves that the French storehouses were empty of gunpowder and everything else. Inevitably, they returned to the Carolinians with whom they had been trading skins and slaves for several years, although Bienville was convinced that they would prefer to do business with the French, if only the French had goods to offer. Even the Carolinians themselves admitted that the Indians loved the French for their "generosity and conversation." But the French could no longer be generous, and conversation was no match for trade goods. In 1704, Carolinian slave traders were back in the Chickasaw villages with their axes, kettles, and woollen blankets, and of course their guns and ammunition, while Bienville waited in vain for supplies from the mother country. Armed with their new weapons, the Chickasaws turned on a group of Choctaws who were paying them a friendly visit, and the captives ended up in the Charles Town slave market. Still, Bienville's diplomatic skills kept some of the Chickasaws in the French alliance. Several Chickasaw chiefs were actually visiting Mobile when word came of the attack on the Choctaws. Since the chiefs could not avoid passing through Choctaw territory on their way home, they asked for an escort past the Choctaw villages, and Bienville selected one of his best officers, Pierre Dugué de Boisbriant, and twenty-five Canadians for the job. At a stopover in a Choctaw village, the hosts returned treachery for treachery by attacking the unsuspecting Chickasaws.

Yet there were signs that the Chickasaws might be willing to reach an accord. According to a French account, thirty Chickasaw chiefs came to Mobile begging Bienville to mediate a peace between them and the Choctaws. Naturally Bienville was only too pleased to comply. The man sent to arrange the peace was again Boisbriant. As soon as Boisbriant arrived at the great Choctaw village of Yomani, the Choctaws reproached him for having any dealings with a people who, they said, had killed Petit Michel, the young Frenchman whom Iberville had left in their village. This the Chickasaws vehemently denied. To prove their point, they sent two runners to their village to retrieve the boy, leaving a few men behind as hostages. When the allotted time passed and neither Petit Michel nor the runners turned up, the Choctaws kept insisting that the Chickasaws were up to their old tricks and that the hostages should be killed, while the hostages protested just as loudly that their runners had likely been murdered by the Choctaws. Here was a fine dilemma for Boisbriant. If he waited too long he might lose his Choctaw allies, and if he allowed the hostages to be killed he would antagonize the Chickasaws. In the end he decided in favor of the Choctaws and the two hostages were killed on the spot. Actually, the Chickasaws had not laid a hand on Petit Michel; the next year he arrived in Mobile safe and sound. Whether the story of the boy's murder was based on rumor or an outright lie on the part of the Choctaws, the incident damaged

French-Chickasaw relations and ended the truce between the two Indian nations.

Yet, Bienville never gave up hope of effecting a settlement, even a temporary one, which would buy a little breathing space until supply ships would arrive from France with trade goods for the proposed new post. In 1706 his efforts were rewarded and he had the pleasure of seeing the Choctaws and the Chickasaws smoke the calumet together. His satisfaction was to be short-lived. Apparently at the instigation of Thomas Welch, the Carolinian trader and explorer, the Chickasaws raided a Choctaw village at night and carried off 150 slaves. In spite of this setback, Bienville was writing in February 1707:

> All these Indians belong to the English only by necessity and interest. They naturally like the French. I have at present two Choctaw and Chickasaw chiefs with me to whom I am showing great friendship, making them hope that we shall go to them [to build the fort] as soon as the vessels from France have come.[2]

The vessels brought little of the hoped-for relief. Matters became so bad that Bienville was forced to use funds earmarked for Indian goods and presents to maintain the garrison. Naturally, Louisiana's scarcity redounded to the advantage of the English. Hitherto, the Carolinians had been content with inciting their own Indian allies to attack the French allies, but knowing of the dearth of provisions in Mobile, they became bolder. They now sought to lure the Choctaws from the French alliance, after which they planned to mobilize all the Indians against Mobile and Pensacola.

Strange as it might appear, considering their superiority in numbers and resources—the combined population of the Carolinas amounted to about 10,000 settlers and about the same number of black and Indian slaves—the English colonists were almost as worried about the French in Louisiana as the French were about them. A small fleet of French privateers aided by Spanish troops from Havana had launched a notably unsuccessful attack on Charles Town in 1706, but rumors were flying of another impending attack, which might be bolstered by assistance from Bienville and his Indian allies. The Carolinians thought that the time was ripe to launch a pre-emptive strike. However, before an attack could be seriously considered, it would be necessary to win over or neutralize all the Indian tribes. In 1708, Carolinian Indian agent Thomas Nairne ventured into the great village of the Choctaws to make peace with them. According to Bienville, the natives

[2]Bienville to Pontchartrain, February 20, 1707, in Dunbar Rowland and Albert G. Sanders, eds. *Mississippi Provincial Archives*, Vol. 2, *1701-1719, French Dominion* (Jackson, Miss., 1927), 37. Hereinafter cited *MPA*.

were shocked at his proposal which was to aid them to destroy all the little nations nearest the fort: the Thomés, Apalachees, Mobiliens, Tensas, Choctaws, Pascagoulas and Pensacolas. Veteran fur trader Thomas Welch went to the Mississippi country, summoned the chiefs of all the river nations—the Yazoos, the Arkansas, the Tunicas, the Tensas, the Natchez and the Koroas—and harangued them to join with him in casting out the French. The gist of his speech was that the nations would be doing themselves a favor, since the Louisianians were nothing but a band of deserters who could expect no help from France.

To counteract the English designs, Bienville put all his powers of diplomacy to work. He entertained native chiefs at Mobile, where they were alternately showered with attention or warned about what might lie in store for them if they lost his friendship and allowed themselves to be manipulated by the Carolinians. In addition, he canvassed his own partisans among the tribes for information about the proposed assault and the disposition of the tribal leaders. By 1708, he judged it safe to make a move. Chateauguay was dispatched to Chickasaw country where he arranged a peace treaty between that nation and the Choctaws. To keep him abreast of any hostile developments, Bienville also sent two young men along, ostensibly to learn the language. With the signing of the treaty, the Chickasaws were neutralized, thus stripping the Carolinians of their main line of offense. For the time being at least, Louisiana could breathe more easily. However, to be on the safe side, he put his men to work strengthening and enlarging the stockade at Mobile and he borrowed ammunition from Pensacola and Vera Cruz. Thanks largely to his clever maneuvering, the first major assault on the colony never got off the ground. That he could rally the tribes together when Carolina had so much more to offer in the way of material rewards is a true measure of his stature among them.

Still the Carolinians continued to incite their allies to make murderous attacks on nations friendly to the French, and in face of repeated slave-raiding forays, small nations such as the Mobiliens were forced to abandon their homelands and move close to Mobile for protection, while the Tunicas and the Houmas fled to the Lower Mississippi. In May 1709, an army of Carolinians, 600 to 700 strong, descended the Alabama River in an attempt to destroy the Mobiliens and the Thomés. At word of the attack, Bienville rushed to the rescue with as many men as he could muster and the invaders abandoned their canoes and took to the woods. At his urging, the French allies pursued them, killed thirty-four men and took five prisoners. Mainly because of his clever maneuvering, the road to Mobile remained blocked, and for the next few years, the Carolinians themselves were too preoccupied with internal disputes to mount another grand-scale attack.

While external threats constantly confronted Bienville, he also had to contend with a host of internal difficulties, some of them of his own making. A mere king's lieutenant without a distinguished career behind him—to say nothing of the fact that he was a colonial—he would have been well-advised to tread cautiously in his dealings with civil and religious authorities. But he was young and brash, and for all his aptitude in Indian affairs he had a lot to learn about domestic politics. Besides, he was a military officer, and like military officers the world over, he expected his orders to be carried out without question. Unable to brook criticism from those he considered meddlers or malcontents, he became embroiled in ridiculous disputes, all of which had deplorable consequences for himself and for the colony.

Of course bickering was nothing out of the ordinary in new colonies. The New England colonies could hardly agree about anything, and bitter in-fighting was the hallmark of Carolinian politics. The French were a particularly contentious lot. In Canada, the governor quarreled with the intendant[3] and sometimes with the bishop; the Recollets had their disputes with the Jesuits; fur traders squared off against rival fur traders, and settlers wrangled about stray cattle. But it was one thing to have squabbling among the higher-ups in a stable colony where ordinary settlers could go about their business without getting drawn into the fray, or even knowing much if anything about it, and quite another thing in a small colony like Louisiana where nothing could be swept under the rug. Everyone knew the twists and turns of the quarrels and everyone took sides, until the colony was split into two opposing factions. Indeed it is difficult to escape the notion that the long-standing duel of words brought a certain excitement into the drab lives of the colonists, even as it undermined their respect for authority.

Part of the problem was the colony's primitive administrative structure. As yet, Louisiana had none of the governing apparatus found in older colonies—no governor embodying the dignity of the king, no intendant responsible for civil affairs, no Sovereign Council to act as a court of justice. Bienville had all the responsibilities of a governor, but not the magic title which would have enhanced his standing in the eyes of the inhabitants. The fact that he had no patronage to dispense as a governor usually did, and no authority to make land concessions also put him at a disadvantage and contributed to the general feeling of uncertainty about his position. As for Nicolas de La Salle, he was merely a scrivener performing the function of commissary; it was Bienville who authorized all expenditures and regulated the consumption of supplies. In times of extreme want, he lowered the official prices, or dipped into one fund to ease

[3]The chief civil administrator.

the burden somewhere else; and when the worst came to the worst, he issued notes on the paymaster of the navy to pay the salaried workers, all of which threw La Salle's records into confusion and gave rise to some lively arguments. His administration of justice also came under fire. Differences between the inhabitants were decided by a military court composed of Bienville and the officers; and since none of these men knew much about the law, the decisions arrived at were not necessarily equitable. As a result, ink flowed very freely to Pontchartrain, complaining about the unfairness of it all.

When word of the very public disputes reached France, Pontchartrain had a few things to say. Probably on the general principle that where there was smoke there was bound to be fire, each party came in for a tongue-lashing, but the brunt of the minister's anger was directed at Bienville, who seemed to be the main culprit. From then on, the young man was kept on a tight rein, and his every move was closely scrutinized.

In theory, Bienville's sphere of action was quite limited. He was expected to send detailed dispatches to Pontchartrain, informing him about conditions in the colony and he could suggest a course of action. All policy decisions were made in France through the navy ministry and he was supposed to follow them, except in emergencies. The trouble was that emergencies requiring immediate action were forever occurring. To await a decision from France would often have been the height of folly, so Bienville frequently acted on his own and justified his actions after the event, which earned him many a sharp rap on the knuckles from Pontchartrain. A bureaucrat in Versailles simply could not understand what Bienville faced. A case in point had to do with the defense of the colony. As an economy measure, the minister sent out orders to disband the Canadians, who formed part of the garrison at Mobile, and to rely solely on French troops. At the risk of incurring the ministerial wrath, Bienville temporized again and again. For all their faults—and they were numerous—the Canadians were indispensable to the safety of the colony. As he told the minister:

> I admit to you, my lord, that I do not know what would have become of this colony if I had dismissed the Canadians. . . . I could do so if I had one hundred and fifty good soldiers. These Canadians are men suitable for everything, on whom one can count, whereas the soldiers and sailors that we are obliged to send to sea desert at the first Spanish land and we find ourselves obliged to employ men at exorbitant prices to bring back the vessels.[4]

[4]Bienville to Pontchartrain, February 20, 1707, *MPA*, 3:38-39.

Bienville also came under fire for his dispensation of justice, Indian fashion. Pontchartrain could not conceive that the summary execution of an Indian who had boasted of killing the missionary, Father St. Cosme, might be the only way to preserve French honor and French lives. Bienville tried to give the Indian perspective on the matter of reprisals:

> Recently the Chickasaw and the Choctaw chiefs asked me in great seriousness if there were really as many men in France as here. . . . I tried to make them understand the truth about the matter by means of striking examples. It was impossible for me to make them believe although I understand their language very well. They gave me as a reason that if there were really as many people as I said, some of them would come here to avenge the deaths of the Frenchmen 'or you have no courage at all'.[5]

Meanwhile, the inhabitants dragged out their lives in utmost misery. As one year followed another with little or no help from France, soldiers deserted at every opportunity, and the regular inhabitants came to believe that the king might abandon the colony altogether. Unable to adjust to the hot, humid weather, they found agricultural work exhausting. To add to their discomfort there were the inevitable hordes of mosquitoes, which swarmed so densely around the marshy ground and stagnant water that they could almost be cut with a knife, according to one newcomer to the colony. Epidemics of malaria and swamp fever brought frequent illness and death, especially to the very young and the newcomers to the colony. When the supply ships from France were delayed, the colonists had to make do with Indian corn, instead of the tasty French bread they loved so much; there were even times when Bienville had to send some soldiers to live among the Indians. As best he could, he tried to rally their flagging spirits: "I assure them," he wrote hopefully to Pontchartrain, "that your lordship will give them assistance in the needs of their establishments and that the war alone is causing them all the hardships that they are suffering."[6]

What Louisiana needed most, as Bienville never tired of pointing out, was an influx of stalwart peasants who would be better able to cope with Louisiana conditions. But it cost too much to send out farmers from France and set them up with animals and tools at a time when the French treasury was empty. Besides, French peasants, poor as they were, were unwilling to risk the perils of an Atlantic crossing to come to an unknown wilderness, rumored to be full of swamps and alligators.

[5]Ibid., 38.

[6]Bienville to Pontchartrain, February 20, 1707, *MPA*, 3:36.

It goes without saying that women considered emigration to the primitive colony to be a fate worse than death. For the first few years, there were only a few French women in the colony: La Salle brought out his wife and children, and apparently there were two or three other families in Mobile in 1703. The rest of the men had no home life at all, although it should come as no surprise to learn that native women hired to do the cooking and housekeeping provided other services on the side. In answer to Bienville's appeals, Pontchartrain agreed to send out a number of girls and provide them with subsistence for a year as the surest way of encouraging the men to settle down and farm the land. This was not a revolutionary idea. It had been tried with great success in Canada; and the English and the Spaniards had tried it in their colonies. The first group of women—and the only group despatched during the war years—twenty-four "young well-raised girls who knew how to work" were chosen by Bishop St. Vallier of Quebec who happened to be in Paris at the time. With an eye to the future, the minister also sent along a midwife, together with a chaperone to look after the girls. What with delays at Rochefort and stopovers in Cap Français and Havana, it took nine months for the unfortunate waifs to reach Louisiana. The voyage itself must have been a nightmare. The cabins, if they had cabins at all, would have been dark and cramped, without decent bedding or sanitary conveniences. After the first few weeks at sea, fresh meat and vegetables probably ran out, leaving the passengers to subsist on dried vegetables and salt meat. Not only that, an epidemic that raged in Havana spread to the ship's passengers, including the women. Unfortunately, the plague brought more havoc in its wake. It spread among the inhabitants of Mobile, carrying off twenty-three men and two women and leaving two-thirds of the garrison weak and ill. Perhaps the greatest loss to the colony was the faithful Henry de Tonty. The man who had survived so many hardships and voyages was unable to withstand the ravages of the fever and he died in Mobile at the age of fifty-four.

On their arrival in the colony, the women found that their new home bore no resemblance to "the Promised Land" that the bishop had led them to expect. Nevertheless, most of them married and settled down, even if their new husbands fell short of expectations. Of course they did have the option of refusing a candidate they did not like, but that was a risky business. Without any means of returning home to France, a single girl who happened to be a bit choosy would have been condemned to the drudgery of a servant's life. Much to Bienville's annoyance, the chaperone, who probably had some money of her own, Marie Françoise de Boisrenaud, rejected all suitors as unworthy of her rank, but when she set her heart on his cousin Boisbriant, it was another story entirely. According to her,

Bienville withheld his consent for the match—perhaps because he disliked her or perhaps because he thought his cousin was too good for *her*!

As far as their moral character was concerned, the new brides were above reproach, but their capacity for hard work fell far below the bishop's assurances. By temperament and upbringing, most of them were quite unsuited to life in a primitive colony. City dwellers all, they were a feckless lot, more interested in "vain show and vanity," said Bienville, than in encouraging their husbands to get down to the laborious business of clearing the ground.

And backbreaking labour it was to try to wrest a living from the land. There were no oxen to speak of—in 1704 La Salle reports a total of four—no plows, and the supply of mattocks, pickaxes and other hand tools was never enough to go around. Even the crops were disappointing. When the inhabitants tried to grow wheat, which they did again and again, it grew wonderfully at first, but when the ear was formed, the crop drooped and eventually withered away. The only crop that grew well was maize, which the men learned to tolerate in time, but the women grumbled a great deal about it.

Contrary to what Pontchartrain was led to believe by some of his correspondents, game was not plentiful in the immediate vicinity of Mobile, and the great heat and scarcity of salt meant that the meat could not be preserved as it was in Canada. Moreover, the Indian hunters who supplied the meat had to be paid in merchandise, which was always in scarce supply. To be sure the unlimited supply of pasture favored cattle raising, so the inhabitants were soon able to sell some dairy produce to the Spaniards at Pensacola. By 1708 the colonists also owned about 2,000 poultry and 1500 pigs; and the gardens supplied beans, peas, and watermelons to supplement the daily diet. But getting the meal on the table was a struggle. So great was the risk of fire in flimsy houses without brick chimneys, that the cooking had to be done in separate kitchens and transported back to the dwellings.

Yet life in Mobile was not all unrelieved gloom. Once in a while there were diversions which revived the traditional buoyancy of the French and brightened their drab lives. A French victory in Europe, or the birth of a French prince was an occasion for general rejoicing, and a visit from the governor of Pensacola was always a gala affair, marked by salvos of artillery and all the pageantry that the colony could muster. Pénigaut describes one such happy event when Governor Don Guzman paid a four-day visit to Bienville. Greeted by a salute from a French honor guard on his arrival, the governor graciously consented to serve as godfather for a new-born infant. The ceremony was conducted "with all desirable pomp," after which Don Guzman had some piastres thrown to the soldiers—more than a thousand, if

Pénigaut is to be believed—and as a special favor he got Bienville to release the prisoners. Every year on the feast of St. Louis, the Apalachees, the only nation of Christian Indians, also put on a celebration for the French. In the morning, the priests and the native congregation chanted High Mass in Latin. Later in the day, the natives presented a masque, followed by feasting and dancing, in which members of both nations took part with gusto.

In 1704, the colony mourned the departure of the Jesuit priest Father Dongé, a gentle soul well-liked by everyone. The new pastor of Mobile was Father Roullaux de La Vente of the Society of the Foreign Missions. Before the year was out, Bienville and La Vente were locked in an unseemly quarrel which degenerated into innuendo and personal attack, and would continue on the same plane until the priest's departure for France six years later.

The dispute between Bienville and La Vente went beyond the personal. Even had Father La Vente been the most accommodating man in the world, he was not a Jesuit, and Bienville had set his heart on having a Jesuit in Mobile. As noted earlier, ties of mutual respect bound the Le Moyne family to the Society of Jesus, and the feeling was strong and lasting. It so happened that Bishop St. Vallier who had jurisdiction over all the French missions in the New World favored the priests of the Foreign Missions over the Jesuits. In part the tension between the two orders stemmed from a decision made by the bishop in 1698, giving the Foreign Missionaries the right to evangelize the Indians in the Upper Mississippi Valley. Immediately a dispute sprang up between them and the Jesuits who already had thriving missions among the Illinois tribes. After the new colony of Louisiana was founded, both orders began intense lobbying for the control of the missions in the Lower Mississippi. To avoid unseemly wrangles between the two orders, the Jesuits asked for their own sector, with their own superior acting as the bishop's vicar apostolic. The bishop refused, and the Jesuits recalled their missionaries from Louisiana, leaving the field to the other priests.

In retrospect, the bishop's decision was probably a mistake. Individually the Seminary priests were zealous men, who took their roles of spiritual and moral leaders very seriously. But the order did not have the resources or the experience of the Jesuits who were engaged in mission work all over the world, from the Far East to the Americas. In working for the glory of God, the Jesuits were also more enterprising and diplomatic than their confrères. As a few commandants and Canadian governors found out, they could be uncompromising when principles were at stake, but they also knew when to turn a blind eye and bide their time. Above all, they always made it their business to learn the Indian languages, something the

Foreign Mission clergy seemed unable to do. Evidence suggests that these priests were never happy in Louisiana. Disappointed with the meagre results of their missionary efforts, the bad climate and poor food, they sank into a kind of lethargy, punctuated by denunciations of the human weaknesses that were all too common in the new colony. Thus, Bienville found himself saddled with priests whom he never wanted in the first place—and what was worse, they soon began to question his authority.

Even before Father La Vente arrived on the scene, the missionary priests were uneasy with the young commandant. They believed that their role as missionaries entitled them to a strong voice on everything pertaining to the native people, while Bienville would have been happier if they stuck to their beads and their breviaries and let him handle Indian policy. Particularly irritating for the priests was the commandant's action—or lack of action—after the murder of one of their number, Father Foucault, the missionary to the Tamaroas. In 1702 the priest and a few companions had been killed in their sleep by their Koroan guides, perhaps for their belongings, or perhaps, as La Harpe says, in revenge for their mistreatment by the French. At all events, Father Davion who worked among the Tunica, fled to Mobile, expecting Bienville to drop everything and avenge Father Foucault's death. Instead of rushing to arms, Bienville temporized for want of sufficient men. Davion was not convinced. He even hinted to his superiors that it was not so much a lack of men as a lack of will, even a lack of courage, that stayed the commandant's hand. If priests were to be killed with impunity, Davion complained, they might as well go home. It is highly unlikely that Father Davion, ordinarily a mild-mannered man who shunned controversy, confronted Bienville to his face, but the atmosphere grew more electric when La Vente arrived on the scene.

Father La Vente came to Louisiana from Bourbon Island in the West Indies. His superiors considered him a wise, industrious, and strongly unselfish man, yet for all his wisdom he spent an inordinate amount of time feuding with the authorities on the island, even if the disagreements were justified by the conditions with which he was faced. No priest worthy of the name could have been expected to tolerate the moral laxity and corruption that he saw all around him. Even so, it must be admitted that Father La Vente allowed his zeal to overcome his judgment. In a situation where common sense might have dictated a certain degree of moderation, he adopted the fire and brimstone approach. Seeing that his efforts met with indifference and downright hostility, he was forced to admit defeat and seek another mission. In July 1704, he arrived in Louisiana to take up the position of pastor at Mobile outside the king's fort.

He had barely set foot in Louisiana before disillusionment set in. It was not one thing he complained about, it was everything. The climate disagreed with him; the food was poor; everything was so extraordinarily dear that he was unable to live on his allowance of 1,000 *livres* a year. He held Bienville to blame for the fact that there was no parish church, and when he did get a makeshift building it was destroyed by storms within a year. Fully expecting Bienville to allocate funds for repairs, he was indignant when the young man insisted there was no such money on hand. As a temporary measure, he said mass in the tiny fort chapel, an arrangement that pleased nobody. It was too small and too noisy for the priest's taste, and the service dragged out so long that it interfered with the garrison's weekly routines.

His proposal for the Indian missions brought him further disappointment. With the few priests that were available, he considered it impossible to make much headway in evangelizing the natives unless they could be induced to give up their wandering ways and assemble in large villages. This resettlement scheme was nothing new. Iberville had proposed an even more grandiose plan for moving the tribes into large establishments for religious and defence purposes. Bienville was also in favor of some regrouping, but as he well knew, regrouping would cost money for gifts, rather lavish gifts, to the tribes affected. He explained the resettlement proposal to Pontchartrain, who was quite receptive at first. Unfortunately, because of the exigencies of the war, the gifts never came, an omission that did not improve Father La Vente's frame of mind.

As time passed, relations between the priest and Bienville became more and more strained. In the best of all possible worlds, the representatives of the cross and the *fleur-de-lis* worked together for the good of all. The commandant, or governor, as the case might be, was expected to be a man of exemplary moral character, a church-goer, and an active supporter of the Church and its representatives. On his side, the priest looked after the moral and religious welfare of his flock, and upheld the governor's authority. It was well understood, nonetheless, that neither power could infringe on the other's territory. But what happened when spiritual and temporal spheres overlapped as they did in the case of public morality? In Canada, Bienville had seen some famous battles between the clergy and the secular authorities about the morality of selling alcohol to the native people. Unaccustomed to the use of liquor, the natives frequently drank to excess and committed crimes they would never have committed when they were sober. While they were in their cups, they were also royally exploited by unscrupulous fur-traders for a few pots of brandy. Seeing the misery and injustice inflicted by the wretched trade, the clergy wanted it banned entirely from the native settlements, while Governor Frontenac and his ilk countered that the natives were just as entitled to liquor as anyone else. Moreover, the governor maintained that if the native allies did not get alcohol in Canada, they would desert in droves to the English colonies where they could get all the rum they wanted. In the long run, the war of words abated, but the issue was never satisfactorily resolved.

In Louisiana, the civil-religious clash occurred not about alcohol sales but about the "scandalous" relationship between French men and native women. Given the fact that French men still outnumbered French women by a ratio of ten to one, it was unrealistic to expect the men to lead monastic lives as long as there were other women around who saw nothing wrong with live-in relationships. This is not to say that adultery was condoned in Indian society, only that unmarried girls were allowed to bestow their favors as they pleased. As far as the French government and the local clergy were concerned, this shameful "debauchery" had to be stopped. But this was easier said than done. Laws or no laws, the soldiers continued to hire native women ostensibly for housekeeping alone; still, children continued to appear who were rather difficult to account for. On the face of it, it would seem that inter-racial marriages should have been permitted and even encouraged. The experiment had been promoted in Canada but without much success: between 1663 and 1700 there were only ten inter-racial marriages in the main colony. More inter-racial unions were formalized in the western outposts, particularly in the Illinois country, where several native women settled down with French husbands after receiving religious instruction and being baptized. In time, however, inter-racial marriages were officially discouraged because the women disliked the constraints of the white man's world.

Nevertheless, when he looked at the "vice" all around him, La Vente urged an end to the ban, particularly when there were children involved. Bienville opposed the unions on the grounds that the women had a habit of leaving their French husbands whenever the fancy took them; and the marriages gave footloose "libertines" an excuse to desert the colony and go off to the wilderness with their Indian relations. He was outraged—or professed to be outraged—about a particularly blatant contravention of church and state law. The priest had secretly blessed the wedding of a "good inhabitant" and a dissolute Indian woman without publishing any banns for fear that the prospective groom's brother, who had declared that he had had unlawful relations with the Indian woman, might oppose this marriage. In contravening the law of the land and the law of the church, Father La Vente could expect a severe reprimand from the minister, or so Bienville probably hoped.

Any possibility of a rapprochement between the priest and the commandant ended in 1706. A baptism was to take place at Mobile, with Bienville as one of the sponsors. In a dramatic and rather cruel way, La Vente humiliated Bienville in front of the entire colony, by refusing to perform the ceremony because the unworthy sponsor had allegedly been carrying on an affair with a French woman. Even if the story was true, which Bienville vehemently denied, it goes without saying that this public affront was not something he was likely to forget. In his next dispatch, he had a curious story of his own to relate about baptisms. Instead of baptizing the children in the usual manner, he told the minister, Father La Vente put them outside the church "entirely naked" for the ceremony, in spite of the remonstrances of his superior, Father Bergier, who was visiting Mobile at the time. The last nine children died immediately of a chill after the ceremony, Bienville informed Pontchartrain. Clothed or naked, the infants would likely have perished anyway, like so many new-born babies in Louisiana. Still, Bienville could only hope that the story would encourage Pontchartrain to replace La Vente with another priest, preferably a Jesuit.

It so happened that the Jesuit priest, Father Gravier, was in Mobile just then in search of medical attention for wounds he had sustained from hostile Indians, and while he was recovering, he acted as chaplain to Bienville and the soldiers at the fort. Behind the move, Father La Vente saw the fine hand of the Jesuits trying to insinuate themselves into his domain. Surely, he wrote, the introduction of Father Gravier was just the thin end of the wedge which would eventually dislodge the Seminary priests from their lawful position in Mobile. Of course there was nothing wrong for a commandant or a governor to have a military chaplain who looked after the spiritual needs of the garrison and took his orders from the commandant. As it happened, however, Fort Louis was too small to house the soldiers, so they lived "outside the king's fort" in the parish of Mobile and technically under Father La Vente's jurisdiction. This being so, La Vente invoked his authority and forbade the Jesuit to give the soldiers their Easter communion. Gravier "for the sake of peace" gave in and shortly after left for France.

The departure of Father Gravier did not, alas, put an end to the quarrels; another actor entered the lists in the person of Nicolas de La Salle. In many respects, the Bienville-La Salle embroglio was nothing more than the usual square-off between a governor and an intendant. On their appointment and at frequent intervals thereafter, these two French officials ordinarily received royal instructions to live in harmony for the good of the colony, but year after year a bundle of mutual recriminations made its way to France. If truth be known, the home government wanted the men to be friendly, but not too friendly. A little mutual spying was all to the good, since it minimized the danger of collusion in far-away colonies.

There was never any danger of collusion between Bienville and La Salle. Undoubtedly there were faults on both sides. Bienville had a good share of the Le Moyne ambition and tenacity, and he could be belligerent and high-handed with those who got in his way. La Salle was an embittered man with a wife and family to support on starvation wages. As we have seen, he had accompanied explorer La Salle on his 1682 expedition to the mouth of the Mississippi, so when the word came out that a colony was about to be established in Louisiana, he felt that his experience entitled him to a position there. No doubt he expected something better than the position he did receive—that of acting commissary which carried a salary of 600 *livres* a year. Pleased that La Salle was bringing out his wife and family to the colony, Iberville petitioned the minister, but without success, to raise the salary. Consequently, instead of bettering himself, the unfortunate La Salle ended up in worse straits than ever. Before leaving Louisiana for the last time, Iberville had had occasion to rebuke La Salle for exceeding his authority, because of his undue "meddling" in the "consumption of supplies and other items." To prevent a recurrence of such behavior, Iberville left orders that La Salle could distribute nothing without the commandant's orders.

A reprimand from Iberville was one thing, but subjection to a young man like Bienville was harder to swallow. Apart from everything else, Bienville's unorthodox financial practices were a sore trial. His habit of juggling funds to meet pressing needs and his incompetence in filling out the necessary records were enough to drive any bookkeeper wild. But La Salle had other and far more serious grievances to report.

The smouldering animosity between the two men did not burst into a conflagration until after Iberville's death in July 1706. By all account, La Salle was a weak man who realized that he had to step very warily while the powerful Iberville was around. Iberville's untimely death could be a blessing or a curse for the commissary. On the one hand, it raised the unpleasant possibility that Bienville would become governor in name as well as in fact. On the other hand, however, it was a heaven-sent opportunity to denounce the Le Moynes, all the more so because Iberville and Sérigny were both suspected of having made illicit gains in the West Indian campaign. To this evidence, La Salle added his own bundle of charges against the Le Moyne brothers. In a thirty-page memoir to the minister, he denounced them right and left. They were no better than rogues who pilfered away his Majesty's goods and effects, he declared. Bienville, in particular, was accused of selling goods to the inhabitants at exorbitant prices, and of keeping for himself the game the Indians brought to Mobile when they came for their presents, whereas the game properly belonged to the royal warehouse. To the charges of corruption, he added complaints of tyranny and cruelty: Bienville had ill-treated La Salle's wife and ordered two Alabama prisoners to be burned in the town square. In other circumstances, Pontchartrain might have taken some of La Salle's allegations with a grain of salt, nothing more than the traditional litany of misdeeds that poured into France from financial officers and military commanders. But the evidence of Iberville's shady dealings, coupled with La Vente's complaints gave them the ring of truth.

Apparently egged on by La Vente, the commissary became more and more insolent. "He was so bold as to tear up an order that I sent to him to have some clothes delivered to an Indian chief," declared Bienville "and he refused to pay several inhabitants what he owed them from the king according to his receipts."[7] When Bienville reproached him, La Salle taunted him by saying that the commandant was in no position to cause any trouble, since he no longer had a patron at the naval ministry.

One of La Salle's charges, and a very serious one at that, was Bienville's unwarranted interference in ecclesiastical matters. Not content with installing the ailing Father Gravier as fort chaplain, as has already been mentioned, Bienville had apparently ordered that the salary attached to the position be paid to the Jesuit. This was a flagrant breach of a formal court order which specified that the salary should go to the Seminary priest Father Huvé who had been appointed chaplain. The same mailbag to France brought Bienville's version of the affair: Father Huvé preferred working with the Indians to working with the garrison, and in fact took off for weeks at a time without a word of explanation. Upon being reprimanded for dereliction of duty, he told Bienville that he was subordinate only to his curate and that he could continue to go where he pleased. Pontchartrain soon disabused Huvé of that idea: if he wanted to be a military chaplain he had to take his orders from the commandant.

And so the deplorable in-fighting continued unabated. The surprising thing is that none of the three main contestants seemed to realize that in casting mud at each other, some of it was bound to stick to themselves. In La Vente's version of events, Bienville was doing his best to make the priests odious to everybody, instead of trying to help them. To hear Bienville tell it, La Vente was a very violent headstrong and deceitful man who publicly told the inhabitants that he [Bienville] was a young man incapable of governing, and that it was foolish to pay attention to him for he would surely be recalled. Were it not that the people had all imaginable confidence in their commandant, Bienville wrote, there might have been a revolt. This hint of clerical insubordination was not likely to please King Louis XIV who was virtually pope within his own kingdom. Then came a counter charge against Bienville which was likely to please the king even less. On a rumor fostered by La Salle, La Vente got word to France that Bienville was intercepting his letters. For lesser charges than mail

[7]Bienville to Pontchartrain, February 20, 1707, *MPA*, 2:41.

tampering, people had been known to find themselves in the Bastille. Meanwhile, the colony was torn apart by the disedifying behavior of its leaders, the Canadians and the officers on Bienville's side, and the malcontents behind La Salle and La Vente.

As Bienville related, in an attempt to curry favor with the ordinary people and discredit him, La Vente put out the word that the commandant was indifferent to their misery. He followed this up by distributing money to the soldiers, giving them to understand that he was continually calling Bienville's attention to their wretchedness but that he was not giving any heed to his pleas. He also humiliated Bienville by writing to Pensacola for flour, charging that the commandant was killing him with starvation, although the flour was really to pay some workmen. "I cannot tell your Lordship the greater part of the harsh things that he says about me," Bienville continued. "In this country where pleasure is unknown we can at least hope for a suitable pastor."[8]

At this point, the normally sanguine Bienville was very discouraged. All his hard work and vigilance had brought him very little in the way of material gain or recognition, he told the minister. On the contrary, his eight years in the colony had retarded his normal advancement in the navy; and his salary of 1,200 *livres* a year was barely enough to keep him for three months. He ended his letter by asking for a year's leave of absence because the hardships of the country and the inclemency of the air had impaired his health.

Back in France Pontchartrain had plans for Bienville that did not include a year's leave of absence for the good of his health. From the mass of conflicting information one thing was clear: the scandal of a commandant feuding openly with a priest and a commissary must not be allowed to continue. In the belief that there was probably blame enough to go around, he curtly advised the Superior of the Foreign Missions that La Vente did not seem to have the qualities necessary for a missionary and probably should be replaced. La Salle was chastised for dereliction of duty in not reporting the colony's accounts and warned that he would have to do better, or face the consequences. But the worst punishment was reserved for Bienville. Nicolas Daneau De Muy, former major of the troops in Quebec, was appointed governor of Louisiana and ordered to investigate the charges against him. Should the charges be upheld, the new governor was empowered to have Bienville arrested and sent to France. Accompanying De Muy was Martin Dartaguiette who would serve as a co-commissary with La Salle and put the colony's financial house in order, but his immediate

[8]Bienville to Pontchartrain, August 20, 1707, *MPA*, 2:44.

function was to be an investigator who would report on everything in the colony and ferret out the truth about Bienville.

Chapter IV
Trials and Conflicts

With the appointment of De Muy, Bienville's authority in Louisiana was over, or so it was intended. Whether the charges against him were substantiated or not, in Pontchartrain's eyes he could not be trusted to guide the colony again. But the best-laid schemes concocted in Versailles had a way of going awry in Louisiana. On the voyage across the Atlantic, De Muy became ill and he died in Havana. Obviously, Bienville could not leave his post, especially as the Carolinians were just then mobilizing their allies for a massive attack on Pensacola, and possibly on Mobile as well, so he continued with the business of enlarging and fortifying the fort as best he could, while Dartaguiette began a formal inquiry into the charges laid against him and his brothers.

The hearing followed the French criminal code of the day. Dartaguiette selected eight witnesses whom he considered the most impartial and questioned them under oath about all they knew regarding the accusations of cruelty, profiteering, misuse of royal vessels, tampering with the mails, and the like. Bienville as the accused was not allowed to be present or to be represented at the hearings, although he had the right to challenge any and all of the witnesses for cause. In fact he did exercise his privilege in the case of four men who might have had a grudge against him for punishments they had incurred for theft, desertion, insubordination, and other offences.

The hearing began on February 24, 1708, and lasted four days. On the whole, the results were quite favorable to Bienville. Almost all the witnesses went out of their way to praise Bienville's leadership and his charity in bad times. Certainly there had been some abuses—even La Salle himself, who was the main accuser, was later found to have diverted large sums to his own account. As for the serious charge of tampering with the mails, one witness after another swore that he had no knowledge of any such action on the part of Bienville. (This fact was later confirmed by a priest of the Foreign Missions, Father Le Maire, who actually saw the disputed letters being transferred to a French ship.) It also appeared that no prisoners were burned in the town square but clubbed to death by the native people, according to the usual native custom.

Dartaguiette's preliminary report to Pontchartrain, while it did raise suspicions of profiteering on the part of the Le Moyne brothers, other officers, and La Salle himself, strongly suggested that much of the evidence against Bienville was thin. In his opinion, the private quarrels between Commandant Bienville and La Salle, had been at the root of many of the changes put forward by the commissary.

Four months later, Dartaguiette's investigation had not turned up much. He was still telling the minister that nothing could equal the dissension between Bienville, on the one hand, and La Salle and La Vente on the other, but that was as far as he went. Nonetheless, the minister still had his doubts about Bienville, and his suspicions led him to make some ludicrous mistakes. Why was Sieur Pailloux holding an army position which the king had granted to the Sieur Monceaux, he asked, and who was this Pailloux, he thundered? As tactfully as possible, Bienville explained that Monceaux had been dead for years, as had been reported long before. Moreover, it was the French authorities, not he, who had appointed Pailloux to the vacant post, so it was not at all on his own authority that he had acted, he concluded. At the risk of offending the minister, he made a half-ironic, half-serious reference to a particularly unsuitable appointment to the garrison:

> Sieur de Valigny, whom your lordship has just sent here by the *Renommé* and whom you order to have serve in the quality of a petty officer appears to be a very fine man. It is a pity that he is maimed. For this country, you know my lord that all one's members are not too many, especially the legs, which are very useful in the detachments which are frequent . . .[1]

(The same Valigny was later reported as quarrelsome and frequently drunk.)

Meanwhile the internal disputes raged on, each side bombarding the French authorities with their versions of the story. It was the same thing all over again: La Salle with his charges of corruption; La Vente complaining about the widespread debauchery of the colonists and the overbearing character of Bienville; and the commandant vigorously defending himself and denouncing both of them. Enraged at the collapse of the case against Bienville, La Salle wrote that Dartaguiette was not deserving of any faith or credit, that he had come to an understanding with Bienville, and that they were both equally bad and corrupt.

As for La Vente, all the influence in the world could not save him after Bienville's next set of accusations:

> M. de La Vente, the curate of this place and superior of the Missions, is keeping an open shop and at higher prices than anybody. He sells a *quart* [quarter cask] quarter cask of brandy for as much as six hundred livres . . . [and] the rest likewise. . . . M. de La Vente sold his flour last year and now . . . he takes it from the King's warehouse . . . which I am

[1]Bienville to Pontchartrain, October 27, 1711, *MPA*, 3:167.

> granting him in order to take from him every reason for saying that I am letting him die of hunger.[2]

By then, Pontchartrain had had enough; a clean sweep was in order. Bienville would remain at his post until a new governor was appointed. At Dartaguiette's discretion, La Salle could be sent home, but the commissary died before any such order could be put into effect. As for Father La Vente, his superiors were told to replace him with a more suitable priest.

Before word of Pontchartrain's decisions reached the colony, La Vente had set sail for France. With the troublesome priest out of the way, the internal quarreling wound down and Bienville was able to devote all his energies to the defence of the colony and the stern struggle for existence. Happily, he was on excellent terms with Dartaguiette, who assured the minister that nobody could be more diligent in the king's service than Bienville.

Both men pressed again and again for more immigrants, good, solid peasants and their wives who would set up permanent establishments in the country. As usual the pleas were in vain. Because the colony had so little to offer, very few people were willing to take the risk of coming to Louisiana, without the initial assistance that the French government was unable to supply. At one stage the minister even thought of sending out pirates from Cartagena. Dartaguiette squelched that idea, arguing that a band of unprincipled scoundrels, even scoundrels with money to spend, would be more trouble than they were worth. Now and then, a few adventurous souls did arrive from France or from Canada on their own—a few artisans and a sprinkling of small merchants, mainly tavern keepers. After making a little money, they would have quit the colony if Bienville had not exerted his right to block their departure. Pontchartrain gave his grudging approval to the decision, followed by a swipe at the commandant: "It is much more advisable", he said "that you should find a way to make them love this country [Louisiana] by a good and prudent government."[3] The truth was that most of the inhabitants would have abandoned the poverty-stricken colony if it had been at all possible.

In those circumstances, it is hardly surprising that agriculture was still neglected. On his return to France in 1712, Dartaguiette estimated that there were only twenty-four families in Louisiana, and of these just four devoted themselves to farming. In the minds of everyone, the best solution to the labor problem was the introduction of black slaves. Year after year, the settlers begged Bienville to put their request to the French government,

[2]Bienville to Pontchartrain, August 20, 1708. *MPA*, 3:137.

[3]Pontchartrain to Bienville, July 11, 1709. *MPA*, 3:128.

and year after year his request went unheeded in France. Not that the French government, or any other government, objected to slavery on moral grounds. The economy of the French West Indies was built on the backs of the slaves, and in 1708 there were already four or five thousand black slaves in South Carolina. Even the clergy added their voices to the chorus, saying that blacks were the only people capable of withstanding the rigors of the hot, humid climate. It was all a question of who would pay for the slaves. Seeing that the colonists could not afford to pay for them, Bienville and Dartaguiette conceived the notion of a barter with the Saint Domingue colony, which was actively looking for Indian slaves at the time, the rate of exchange to be one black for every two Indians. This scheme flew in the face of Bienville's own ban on Indian slave trafficking, and the minister forbade it.

Of course the colony had a number of Indian slaves from the beginning. In accordance with the native custom, some of these slaves were given to the French to cement alliances, some were prisoners from hostile tribes, and some came in exchange for one favor or another. Nevertheless, a working slave trade never existed in Louisiana, although some unscrupulous *voyageurs* were not above taking the law into their own hands when they thought they could get away with it. St. Denis had to be taken to task for just that; and Bienville's own nephew, a young scapegrace named Jacques de St. Hélène lost his life in a slave-trading expedition. Bienville policed the activities as best he could. He confiscated the slaves and sent them back home and forbade these *voyageurs* to trade for any more from any nation whatsoever, he told the minister. The Indian slaves that were acquired in one way or another were just as averse to hard manual labour as the French, besides having a tendency to run away. For the most part, the men worked in the gardens or cut planks and, as we have seen, the women did regular household chores for the soldiers in the garrison. After repeated complaints from Father La Vente, Bienville ordered the soldiers to send the women to sleep in houses where there were French women. However, he was hardly in a position to be too dogmatic about it, or the men might desert. As it was, several soldiers, weary of their miserable conditions, did desert to the Spaniards and even to Carolina, and others disappeared into the woods. When called into service at Mobile, St. Denis, who was a "voluntary" officer simply sent word to Bienville that he did not want to serve the king any more because he had not been paid. Displeased though he was, Bienville could hardly blame him for his decision.

Of all the people in the colony, the soldiers suffered the worst hardships. "It is pitiful to see them," wrote Dartaguiette, "as they are all naked and most of them living on crushed corn and a piece of meat."[4] When their uniforms were worn out, the unfortunate men were forced to make their own clothes out of deerskins, which naturally damaged French prestige among the Indians. As yet, they had no barracks, so Bienville "obliged them to make barracks for themselves in groups of six" and he was forever begging for bedding and clothing, with little result. Their misery was further aggravated by the fact that they had no hospital and nobody qualified to look after them when they were ill; Bienville earned himself a sharp reprimand for trying to force the midwife Marie Grisot to help care for the sick men. Their pay was often in arrears, and when it did come it amounted to about eighteen *livres* a year after deductions were made for food and clothing. Things got so bad in the summer of 1710 that Bienville was obliged to call in some friendly chiefs and ask them to quarter thirty-five soldiers among them. In their absence he was left with only thirty men to guard the colony from outside attack.

Later that year an attack was mounted on Dauphin Island. Previous warnings from Bienville, reiterated by Dartaguiette, that it was "absolutely essential" to fortify Port Dauphin with a solid stone fort had gone unheeded. That the little wooden stockade hastily thrown together in 1709 was of little use against an invader became obvious when an English privateer from Jamaica swooped down on the island in September 1711, burned the king's warehouse and pillaged all before him. "This loss," wrote Dartaguiette, "has brought this poor colony within two finger breadths of ruin and I can assure your Lordship that it amounts to eighty thousand piastres."[5]

Meanwhile, it became obvious that the colonists at Mobile would have to cast around for a new site. Always subject to spring floods, an unprecedented overflow in 1710 swamped the town and drowned out the crops. The following year, the settlers dismantled their homes, packed up their few belongings and slipped down the river to the site of the present Mobile, Alabama. There, in a place better protected from flooding, Bienville planned the new Fort Louis. The settlers, with the help of the Apalachee Indians set to work with a will.

> The entire colony appears to be very much pleased with the change that we have made and each one is working in emulation of the others on his private establishment. There now remains at Fort Louis only five or six houses which are preparing to come down to the new establishment immediately.[6]

[4]Memoir of Dartaguiette to Pontchartrain, May 12, 1712, *MPA*, 2:60-61.

[5]Dartaguiette to Pontchartrain, January 10, 1711, *MPA*, 2:69n.

[6]Bienville to Pontchartain, October 27, 1711, *MPA*, 3:162.

The new Mobile was very much like the first. Dotted here and there along the parallel streets were little one-storey houses, many of them surrounded by vast gardens, roughly 75 feet by 150 feet. The houses were constructed of cedar and pine, filled in "with a kind of plaster made from earth and lime" on a foundation of wooden stakes to prevent the water from seeping in. The fort itself was outside the town close to the river bank and surrounded by a row of stakes enclosing a storehouse, a guardhouse, and a house, as yet unfinished, for the governor.

In fact, a new governor had been appointed in 1710 in the person of Antoine de La Mothe Cadillac, the former commandant of Fort Detroit. Instead of coming down the Mississippi as had been expected, Cadillac dilly-dallied for a year in Canada on one pretext or another before departing not for Louisiana, but for France. While he was there, momentous events were taking place in Europe. The War of the Spanish Succession was winding down, and France was casting around for some way to ease the financial burden for the Mississippi colony. A potential savior appeared on the scene, a wealthy merchant named Antoine Crozat, to whom the king was willing to cede the colony for a period of fifteen years. In return for all the mineral rights and an exclusive trade monopoly, Crozat was expected to develop the population and resources. While Crozat was still debating about whether to accept the offer or not, Cadillac put all his powers of persuasion to work. In a memoir to Crozat, he painted a glowing picture of the immense riches of Louisiana, its mines of gold and silver, its pearls and its minerals. These visions of a new El Dorado were enough to dissipate the financier's qualms and the contract was signed a few months later.

Other changes were also in store for Louisiana. Jean-Baptiste Duclos was appointed commissary general, and arrangements were made to end military rule in the colony by establishing a judicial council to be composed of Cadillac, Duclos, Bienville and three colonists. In the new regime, Bienville would be commandant of the Mississippi Basin, where he would oversee the construction of new posts and keep the native people at peace with each other and with the French. The appointment was a tacit endorsement of Bienville's Indian policy, but it was a demotion nonetheless. In his first letter to Pontchartrain after hearing of Cadillac's appointment, his bitterness shows:

> I have been here for thirteen years; I have spent my youth here; I have worn out my health here and I have not, my lord, certainly made any profit here. Far from that, I have been obliged to contract debts, as it would be easy for me to prove to you in order to meet expenses. . . . Permit me therefore, my lord, to call your attention to the fact that I have not yet received any favor, that I am only a naval guard, that I

> have not amassed any property at all here and that my labors have not yet procured me any advancement in the navy . . . in which I see many of those who have come after me far advanced, who have not by a great deal endured the hardships that I have had since I have been here, one day on Indian corn, another on wheat and often without either. It has been seven years since I received one sou of my salary, which is very moderate and which would not even be enough to receive the Indians who drop in to see me every day. . . . If you had any kindness for me, my lord, I should hope that you would be so good as to do me the favor of increasing my salary and of granting me a commission of captain of a fireship or lieutenant of a vessel with the Cross of St. Louis which gives great distinction here both among the Indian nations and among the Spaniards. . . .[7]

His pleas fell on deaf ears: there would be no raise in salary, no military advancement, no Cross of St. Louis, he was told, until the king was sure he deserved them. For the present, he was warned to hold himself in "strict subordination" to the new governor. The old list of charges was also dredged up again and given to Cadillac to investigate.

Dartaguiette returned to France in November 1711. During the following eighteen months before members of the new regime put in an appearance, Louisiana was left to muddle along on its own, just when it was facing an onslaught on its borders. For a long time, the Carolinian House of Assembly had been debating about when and how to resume the offensive which had fallen through in 1708. In May 1711, the Assembly decided on a two-pronged approach: first, they would break up the Choctaw-Chickasaw alliance which Bienville had been fostering for years, after which they would destroy the Choctaw nation, the bastion of Louisiana.

Taking advantage of Louisiana's straitened circumstances, the Carolinians showered the Chickasaws with gifts and persuaded them to renew their old feud with the Choctaws. Interpreters from some Chickasaw tribes still friendly to the French got word to Bienville that a massive expedition consisting of sixty Englishmen and 3,000 Indians was mustering to attack the Choctaws, an undertaking which could spell disaster for the French, for without the Choctaws, the French would have no allies worth mentioning. "If the Choctaws who serve as a rampart for us once happen to be destroyed," Bienville told Pontchartrain, "we should be in a very insecure position."[8] Forewarned of the attack, the Choctaws put up what resistance they could. An army of over 1,000 Creeks led by Captain Theophilis

[7]Bienville to Pontchartrain, October 27, 1711, *MPA*, 3:168-69.

[8]Bienville to Pontchartrain, October 27, 1711, *MPA*, 3:160.

Hastings with a supporting group of Chickasaws under Indian agent Thomas Welch killed over 100 Choctaws, carried off 150 prisoners, and put 400 homes to the torch. But it did not succeed in its main objective—to exterminate the Choctaws and clear the path to Mobile.

The following year a French prisoner who had managed to escape from Carolina brought word of a projected land and sea attack on Mobile and Pensacola. The Carolinians had also questioned the prisoner about the situation in Louisiana, whether the Indian allies could be bribed by large presents, and whether the soldiers in the garrison were so wretched that they would lay down their arms in the event of an attack. The prisoner's story was confirmed by an escapee from Alabama, who told Bienville about an arms build-up on the Alabama River. Taking advantage of a ship bound for Saint Domingue, Bienville got a message to Pontchartrain. Typically, he moved swiftly to avert the threat, never once allowing it to dampen his self-confidence:

> I do not think my lord, that I ought in prudence to give in detail the present situation of the colony in view of the fact that the passage of this small vessel is not at all safe since it has a crew of only 12 men and passes by some English cruisers. I shall only assure your Lordship that I am taking all the necessary measures in order to resist thoroughly the success of this enterprise. It will not be so easy as they think to make themselves masters of this colony.[9]

Bienville's talent for diplomacy once again saved the day. He managed to win over the Alabamans, who held the key to the border with Carolina, after which he moved to engineer a truce between the surrounding nations and his own allies. With this stroke of genius, the whole anti-French coalition collapsed. For the second time, an English scheme to foment a general uprising against the French came to nothing.

Towards the end of the War of the Spanish Succession, Bienville also had to tread warily in his dealings with his Spanish neighbors. Of course there had always been a hint of uneasiness in Franco-Spanish relations. By the end of the seventeenth century, Spain was a ghost of her former self. While it resented the French presence in Louisiana, on land which it considered part of its own empire, it was quite unable to enforce its claims. Still the viceroy of New Spain kept a sharp eye out for any French intrusion westward toward Mexico or east of the Mobile River. On his side, Bienville had his orders not to provoke a quarrel, but to try "adroitly" to extend the French boundaries. He often had "little discussions" with the

[9]Bienville to Pontchartrain, March 2, 1712, *MPA,* 3:172.

governor of Pensacola on the subject, the governor claiming all the land up to the Mobile River and Bienville using the Perdido River as the dividing line. But whatever their differences, the two powers maintained a united front in the face of the English—a kind of marriage of convenience based on mutual fears of English aggression and on the solidarity between Louisiana and Pensacola, where the threat was as grave for one as it was for the other.

The fact was that neither Pensacola nor Louisiana could have survived without the other's help. Time and time again each colony was forced to buy or borrow food and ammunition from the other, and the people of Pensacola were glad to obtain fresh vegetables and dairy products in return for specie which Louisiana sorely lacked. For all that, Bienville and the governor had their differences. It rankled the governor that Bienville was able to attract so many Indian tribes, particularly the Apalachees, to the French alliance. After a Carolinian assault decimated the Apalachian villages near the Spanish stronghold of St. Augustine in 1704, the survivors left their former allies and fled to Louisiana. "From all these Apalachee Indians there escaped only 400 persons who have returned to take refuge on our river and have asked me for permission to plant crops and to make a village there," Bienville wrote.[10] From that point on, the Apalachees, sedentary Indians who had learned how to farm from the Spanish missionaries, remained faithful to the French, and since they were converts to the Catholic religion there was never any fear that they would go over to the English.

The dispersal of the Apalachees from their former homeland left Pensacola particularly vulnerable to Carolinian attack and the attacks were not slow in coming. On each occasion, Bienville sent the governor all the men and ammunition he could spare. In 1708, hearing that a Carolinian army had reached the gates of Pensacola, he set out himself with an army of soldiers and Indians to come to the governor's aid. By the time he arrived, the enemy had retired, partly because they had been warned of Bienville's approach, but chiefly because of dissension in the ranks. The inhabitants of Pensacola were delighted to see Bienville and his allies come to their aid, as he told Pontchartrain. Delighted or not, the governor took the occasion to again reproach Bienville for having attracted Indian tribes away from Pensacola and commanded him on behalf of the viceroy to send them back. This bluster was hardly something that worried Bienville, knowing as he did that the Indians would never be induced to return to the Spaniards whom they heartily disliked.

He was worried, however, that Dauphin Island could very easily fall into Spanish hands. As early as 1707, he was telling the minister:

[10]Bienville to Pontchartrain, September 6, 1704, *MPA,* 3:29.

> Because of the false reports that are often current in the ports of New Spain that we shall soon have war with them I think myself obliged, my lord, to call your attention to the fact that it is absolutely necessary to fortify the port of Massacre [Port Dauphin] since we are at the door of Spain. They could come overnight and seize the port and blockade us here so that we should not be able to receive any assistance by sea.[11]

As we have seen, his worries about Port Dauphin were only too well-founded, but the attack came from a different direction.

Even if Spain had neither the will nor the power to oust the French from Louisiana, there is good reason to believe that as the war progressed the Spanish colonies were ordered not to go out of their way to assist the colony. They were slower to help out in emergencies and when they did respond they acted with such bad grace "that it would have to be a matter of having no supplies at all before their aid would be sought." They also became more rigid about prohibiting French ships from entering Spanish ports in the Gulf of Mexico. In 1711, the royal officers at Vera Cruz went so far as to confiscate a cargo of linens, laces, and other items from Louisiana which Bienville had hoped to barter for food. Even though the Spaniards were quite within their rights according to the letter of the law, this was scarcely the treatment accorded an ally. In fact, in a few years Spain and France would be locked in a war which would have repercussions in Louisiana.

Despite the hardships of the war years, Louisiana managed to survive. Through Bienville's maneuvering, the Chickasaws were kept at bay and the Choctaws remained loyal allies. To be sure, some Carolinian traders were edging their way toward the Mississippi, but for all their efforts, the English colonies failed to destroy the puny little settlement or to establish a post on the river. And the cessation of hostilities in Europe allowed the colonists to hope that the king would be in a position to come to the assistance of the colony that bore his name.

[11]Bienville to Pontchartrain, February 20, 1707, *MPA*, 3:39.

Chapter V
The Crozat Regime

It is probably fair to say that Bienville would have resented any governor appointed to replace him, but Cadillac was an easy man to resent. Ever since his arrival in Canada in 1684 as an obscure immigrant, he had been embroiled in controversy; and there is a wealth of evidence to suggest that he never let honesty or truthfulness get in the way of his progress. The governor of Acadia called him the greatest liar that ever lived and the same judgment was later to be made by Commissary Duclos. Even his name was a fiction. He was not the Sieur de La Mothe Cadillac that he gave himself out to be, but plain Antoine Laumet, the son of a rural magistrate. Nevertheless, his smooth tongue and talent for self-promotion brought him to the attention of the two people who mattered, Navy Minister Pontchartrain and Louis de Buade de Frontenac, then governor of Canada. Through Frontenac's influence, Cadillac became military commander of the fur-trading settlement at Michilimackinac, where his talent for managing the Indian tribes was far surpassed by his ability to make money in the illegal brandy trade. Later, as founder and commandant of Detroit, his bumbling administration had achieved the very thing it was supposed to prevent: rather than uniting against their common enemies as he had predicted, the Indian allies around the new settlement were battling one another and deserting the French. As for himself, he was feuding with the Jesuits, the merchants, the settlers—in a word, with everybody. He was even refusing to carry out the orders of Governor Vaudreuil. When the complaints about his mismanagement could no longer be ignored, Pontchartrain sent out a government official named Clairambault d'Aigremont to investigate. The report was a biting indictment of the man and his policies. Not only was he hated by everyone, the document concluded, but his policies could be the ruin of the colony.

With this report in his hand Pontchartrain had little choice but to recall Cadillac, but to recall his protégé was as good as admitting that he himself had made a mistake in supporting him for so long. According to a memoir of the day, the appointment to Louisiana was not so much a promotion as a pretext to get him out of Detroit. So to rid himself of a troublesome embarrassment, Pontchartrain delivered Louisiana into the hands of a known bungler. How the king could say with a straight face that he expected the turbulent Cadillac to govern the Louisiana inhabitants justly, mildly, and disinterestedly, to maintain them in union and peace, and procure for them the greatest possible accommodation is a mystery.

On the voyage to Louisiana, Cadillac began to show his real colours. By trying in turn to cajole and intimidate Duclos, a young man without colonial experience, he hoped to get his hands on the royal funds, which were controlled by the commissary. However, his never-ending boasting about all the battles he had fought and won—all because of his "superior mind"—only served to turn Duclos against him. As for Duclos' opinion of the "superior mind:"

> He [Cadillac] appeared to me in fact a very dangerous man not because of the superiority of his mind which I did not find superior except where his interest is concerned . . . and furthermore . . . he was one of the boldest liars I have ever seen.[1]

Six months after his arrival in Louisiana, Duclos was asking to be recalled because Cadillac was too crafty for him.

As soon as he set foot in the colony, Cadillac began to criticize everything and everybody. The country was "useless," the people were "the dregs of humanity," addicted to vice with Indian women, the officers knew nothing about the service, the soldiers were undisciplined, and the clergy were too strict. The higher-ups fared no better. One of Crozat's agents was a libertine, another one was a fool, Duclos was dishonest, and Bienville applied himself solely to his own affairs, leaving everything in utter confusion.

One of Cadillac's jobs, which he pursued with some relish, was to investigate the old charges against Bienville. In a few months he had dredged up a great deal of gossip about him, which he relayed to Pontchartrain, all the while insisting that he did not intend "to condemn" Bienville out of hand. To confuse the issue for the minister, the same mailbag brought a dispatch from Duclos praising Bienville, and accusing Cadillac of all kinds of trickery and mismanagement. Apparently Duclos also refused to cooperate with Cadillac in any formal investigation of Bienville, saying that it was a trifling matter, that the affair was too old and based chiefly on La Salle's unsupported word. In the end, Cadillac was forced to let the investigation drop, but not before he had succeeded in alienating Bienville for good.

What especially galled Cadillac was Bienville's influence with the native people, who made a habit of going to him with their troubles as they had done in the past. He also resented the fact that Bienville had the authority to disperse half the money allotted for presents to the Indians. It must also be said that Bienville made no attempt to hide his contempt for Cadillac, whom he considered a pompous fool. In one altercation, which Cadillac reported word for word to Pontchartrain, he contradicted the

[1]Duclos to Pontchartrain, October 13, 1713, *Louisiana Historical Quarterly*, 27 (1934): 269.

governor to his face and ended up under house arrest for a day. Not at all chastened, Bienville retorted that he was only too happy to have a day indoors, now that the hot season had arrived.

The subject of Crozat's monopoly gave rise to more dissension. The financier was not in business for the good of his health or to build a fine colony, but to make money, and his buy-low, sell-high policy worked havoc on the poor inhabitants and stifled any economic life. Added to this, by the terms of the monopoly, the people were forced to trade at the company stores, where they were reimbursed in high-priced goods, not cash. Forbidden to take their vegetables, poultry and their few other paltry products to Pensacola, as they had been in the habit of doing, the colonists, who had been led to believe that the end of the war would bring them some relief, found themselves in worse straits than ever. In the face of this hardship, they took every opportunity to smuggle their merchandise to Pensacola where they were well paid in piastres; and very soon they were openly condemning the whole idea of a monopoly.

Increasingly, Bienville and Duclos spoke up for the inhabitants, while Cadillac naturally sided with the Company, in which he had a small share. He also did his best to foster Crozat's two main money-making schemes—exploiting the mines and trading with the Spaniards in Mexico. Neither Duclos nor Bienville had any faith in Spanish trade, by land or by sea. Apart from the great distance involved and the danger of an attack from hostile tribes, the viceroy of New Spain had made it very clear that he wanted no traffic with the French. Still Cadillac sent a ship loaded with merchandise to Vera Cruz, only to have it sent back without selling a single item.

An unofficial land expedition to the Red River under the command of Juchereau de St. Denis fared no better. Most of the men had to return without selling their wares because of the hostile tribes on the way, but the venturesome St. Denis and his Natchitoches guides pushed on. Upon reaching the ancient Natchitoches homeland on the Red River, St. Denis assembled the chiefs, distributed grain among them, and told them to cultivate their fields and rebuild their village. Leaving a few of his own men with them, he assured the natives that French people would come and live in their midst. This tiny outpost on the Red River was the first step in establishing French control over the western limit of the Mississippi Valley. St. Denis's subsequent adventures are the stuff of legend. After making his celebrated trek across East Texas with a string of mules, he was twice thrown into Spanish prisons and eventually married the granddaughter of the Spanish commandant at Presidio de San Juan Bautista, the Spanish post on the Rio Grande. Two years later, he was back in Louisiana with his wife and child, but with nothing for the coffers of the Company.

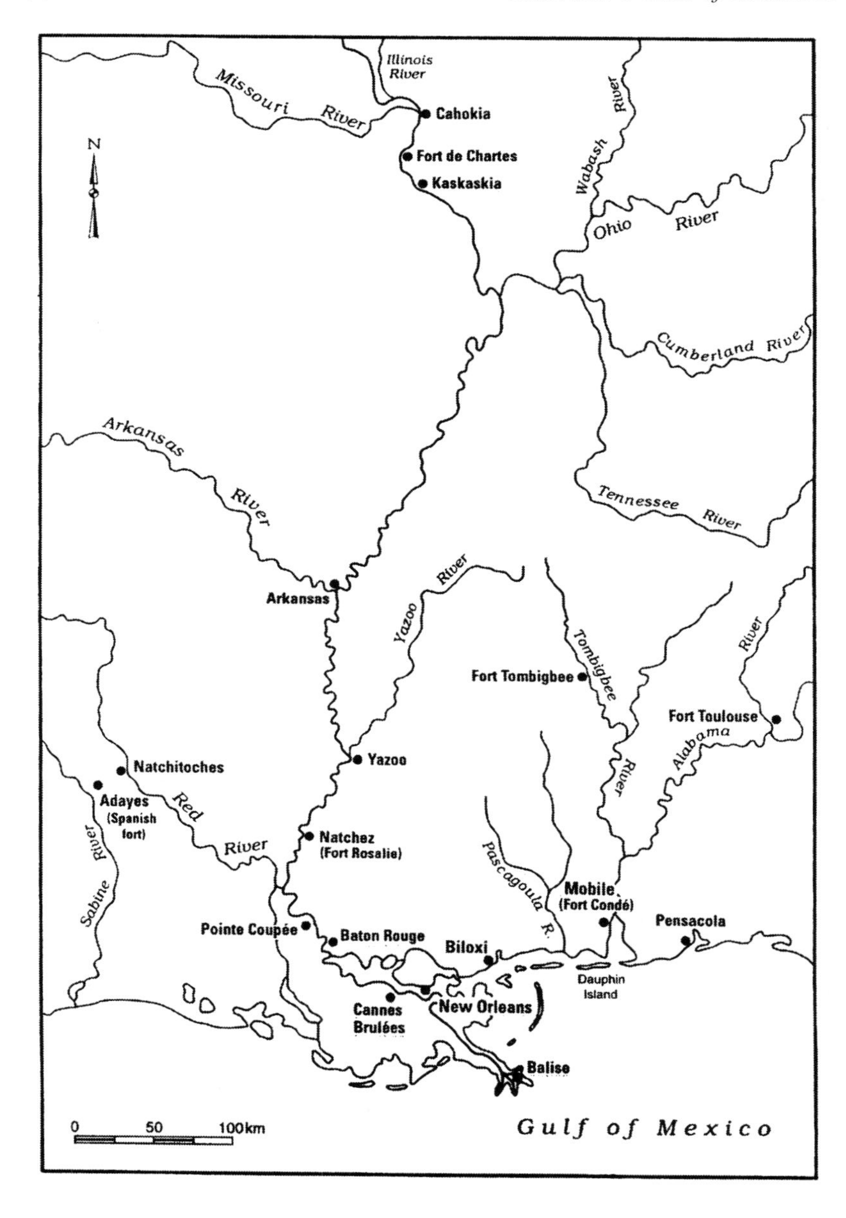
Illinois River
Missouri River
Cahokia
Fort de Chartes
Kaskaskia
Wabash River
Ohio River
Cumberland River
N
Arkansas River
Tennessee River
Arkansas
Yazoo River
Tombigbee River
Fort Tombigbee
Fort Toulouse
Alabama River
Natchitoches
Yazoo
Adayes
(Spanish fort)
Red River
Sabine River
Natchez
(Fort Rosalie)
Pascagoula R.
Mobile
(Fort Condé)
Pensacola
Pointe Coupée
Baton Rouge
Biloxi
Dauphin Island
Cannes Brulées
New Orleans
Balise
0 50 100km
Gulf of Mexico

Meanwhile Cadillac's bumbling treatment of the native people was threatening to undermine Bienville's painstaking system of alliances. He offended chiefs by posting a sentinel at his door and refusing to allow them to enter unannounced, whereas Bienville was in the habit of letting them come and go at will. Rather than laboring long and hard to settle their disputes, as Bienville had always done, his attitude was the more squabbles the fewer Indians. All in all not a bad thing, in his opinion. One misstep after another helped to drive the tribes into the arms of the Carolinians, who were readying themselves for another aggressive push into the Mississippi Valley.

Fortunately for the survival of the colony, Cadillac set off to the Illinois country in the spring of 1715 to look for silver mines. Left on his own, Bienville moved immediately to repair fences. Knowing how much the chiefs disliked Cadillac, he called them together and told them that the governor was gone for good. At his urging, the Choctaws arrested an English trader and plundered a storehouse of presents destined for the Mississippi tribes allied to the French, contrary to the spirit of the Treaty of Utrecht which enjoined English and French colonists to stay out of each other's zones. A little later, Marc-Antoine Loire des Ursins, Crozat's storekeeper at Natchez, and a few Canadian traders captured another prize, Price Hughes, the man behind the grand plan to found English settlements up to and beyond the Mississippi River. During the three days that Hughes was detained in Mobile, Bienville confronted him about his intrigues among the Indian tribes, in violation of the terms of the treaty binding France and England not to molest each other's Indian allies, or incite them to revolt. To which Hughes cooly replied that the English could claim the territory too. Hughes had a point. The Treaty of Utrecht which ended the War of the Spanish Succession, did not lay down the exact boundaries between the French and English colonies or determine which tribes should be attributed to either country, decisions which were left to a subsequent commission to decide. In Bienville's view, the only way to put a stop to the English aggression was to have the boundaries between Carolina and Louisiana settled once and for all. To back up his argument he sent Pontchartrain a copy of Hughes's commission setting forth the English claims to all the lands up to the Spanish border, but nothing came of his efforts.

On his way home to Carolina, Price Hughes was waylaid and killed near Pensacola by a party of Thomé Indians. Already a far-reaching revolt against the tyranny of the Carolinian traders was under way. "Notoriously infamous for their wicked and evil actions," lawless traders had been cheating the Indians, taking their peas and watermelons without leave, treating the men like beasts of burden, and debauching the women. During the two-year uprising known as the Yamasee War, several tribes including the Creeks, the Alabamans, the Cherokees, and the Choctaws mustered in a body against the Carolinians. After killing several traders, the armies advanced on the settlements, slaughtering and capturing numerous settlers and black slaves. As usual Bienville acted with despatch to capitalize on the situation. French envoys were sent out to the Creeks and the Alabamans, and by the end of the year all the tribes were once more smoking the calumet with the French. At the same time, he was careful to do nothing that might provoke the Carolinians to attack the colony. He did the best he could to rescue any English prisoners from the Indians and have them brought to safety in Mobile, where they were well treated until an English ship picked them up several months later.

The insurrection and his deft handling of events succeeded in enlarging French influence over the tribes, although Bienville was realistic enough to know that the alliance would break up unless he had more trade goods and a post on the strategic Alabama River.

In October 1715, Cadillac was back in Mobile. He had very little to say about mines in the Illinois country, but (understandably) a lot to say about Bienville's presumption in representing himself to the Indians as the true governor. Perhaps from personal pique, he made the inexcusable mistake of vetoing Bienville's request to build the Alabama post, thus making it easy for the English to regain the ground they had lost in the Yamasee War. Meanwhile, on his own travels he had managed to antagonize the Natchez, a powerful nation who lived in the vicinity of the present Natchez, Mississippi.

In some ways, the Natchez were quite unlike other Indians. The nation was an autocracy, with a rigid caste system, consisting of the nobility, known as the Suns, and the common people, or Stinkards. The overall chief named the Great Sun had absolute power over his subjects, and less important Suns ruled over individual villages. When Iberville visited the Great Village in 1700, he was struck by the power and authority of the Great Sun, the "most absolute Indian" he had ever seen. He was less impressed with the ritual mass strangulation that occurred on the death of the Great Sun in order that the chief might have an escort into the next world. The Natchez were farmers first and hunters second. On their fertile land, dotted with lush vegetation, they harvested fruit, vegetables, and especially maize. Their most sacred celebration of the year was the Great Corn Feast in late fall.

For the first decade of its existence, the French colony had very little contact with the Natchez. However much they were impressed by the rich soil and pleasant climate in the region—and there is no doubt that they were impressed—with only a handful of men in the colony, a settlement so far from Mobile was out of the question. However, its strategic position on the river encouraged Crozat to open a trading post in the Natchez territory in 1714. Bienville was also ordered to establish a military post in the area, but the construction had to be postponed for lack of soldiers to guard it.

For a year or so, everything seemed to go well enough at Crozat's trading post—that is until Cadillac appeared on the scene. As a contemporary chronicle relates, on his way to the Illinois to look for mines, he passed by the Natchez villages without bothering to stop, and on his way back, he picked up supplies and immediately went on his way, neglecting to pay the usual courtesy call on the Great Sun. This inexcusable breach of etiquette on the part of the French chief, especially when the Natchez were celebrating the Great Corn Feast, led the natives to believe that the French were no longer their friends. In reprisal for the perceived insult, the Natchez fell on four *voyageurs*, stripped them of their goods to the tune of 10,000 *livres* and put the men to death.

Quite oblivious of the trouble he had stirred up, Cadillac returned to Mobile and ordered Bienville to set off for Natchez territory without delay to build the new fort. As Bienville well knew, that would be a difficult task with the forty raw recruits assigned to him for the job. When word of the Natchez attack reached Mobile, Bienville was instructed to avenge that atrocity as well, but instead of getting more men for the job, his contingent was reduced to thirty-six, so that he believed, perhaps not without reason, that Cadillac wanted him to fail and become discredited.

It was no mean task for an impoverished colony to outfit and provision the soldiers, and supply them with boats for the long journey to Natchez territory. While Bienville was doing his best to oversee the preparations, Cadillac was showering him with unnecessary and contradictory advice, but little in the way of material support. As Bienville reported to Pontchartrain:

> I do not have a single soldier who is acquainted with the country and who has ever fired a shot with a musket. They are all raw recruits. I shall even be greatly embarrassed to have them clear a tract of land and build on it a fort, some barracks to lodge them, a warehouse, a chapel, a powder magazine [and] a house for the officers, the chaplain and myself, and no funds at all are given to me for all that. I shall not even have a blacksmith to repair the axes and other tools.[2]

For all that, he told the minister that he was confident of success.

On February 15, his little army set off to face what could well be a hostile force of 800 strong. From Mobile the army traveled westward to

[2]Bienville to Pontchartrain, January 2, 1716, *MPA*, 2:195.

Lake Pontchartrain and Lake Maurepas and thence to Bayou Manchac which took them to the Mississippi. Three months later they reached the land of the Tunicas, ordinarily staunch allies of the French. There some bad news awaited them. The missionary to the Tunicas, Father Davion, had left a letter in a tree with the information that another Frenchman had been killed at the hands of the Natchez; and what was more alarming, the Natchez were said to be urging the Tunicas to attack the French contingent.

Obviously the situation called for a cool head. Instead of proceeding to the Tunica village, Bienville decided to set up camp on an island some distance away, after which he oversaw the construction of a prison, a guardhouse, and a supply depot. In the meantime, one of his best *voyageurs* was dispatched upriver to place warning signs at various intervals for unsuspecting travellers with the message: "The Natchez are at war with the French, and M. de Bienville is camped at the Tunicas." When all this was completed, he launched his plan for dealing with the Natchez without waging a war which he knew he could not win.

Pretending that he knew nothing about the murders, he sent a message to the Natchez village eighteen miles away saying that he would like to speak to the leaders. Three days later a few members of the lower nobility presented themselves to smoke the calumet. This he refused to do, saying that as the French chief, he would smoke only with the Suns. The envoys had no recourse but to return to their village, while Bienville waited for the next developments.

About a week later his scouts brought word that a fleet of pirogues was approaching the landing place. At once, Bienville had half of his men hide in the guardhouse. The remainder grouped around him, their arms at the ready. On disembarking, the leaders, who were lesser Suns, confidently proffered the calumet, in the belief that Bienville was coming merely to build a fort. Instead, Bienville curtly refused the calumet and demanded to know why the Natchez had killed the *voyageurs*. At this unexpected show of anger on Bienville's part, the great priest turned his face to the sun, invoking the god to make the French chief more merciful. To no avail. Since they had no explanation to offer, Bienville had them thrown into the new jail.

Next day the three great chiefs, the Great Sun, the Little Sun, and Stung Serpent appeared on the scene. Bienville began by assuring the chiefs that he did not hold them responsible for the murders of the Frenchmen; on the other hand, he insisted that the murderers would have to be executed. Did they not know that he himself adhered to the native custom in his dealings with Indians and French alike, he asked? At his insistence, Little Sun was sent back to the Natchez village to seek out the guilty men. The next day he returned with three heads, and presented the grisly offerings to Bienville, who discovered that one belonged to a man who had nothing to do with the crimes. At that, Bienville reproached Little Sun for killing an innocent man. It was then that the Great Sun and Stung Serpent confessed to Bienville that the Natchez nation was split into two opposing camps, one faction to which the offending chiefs belonged being in favor of an alliance with the English. Two of the chiefs were in the French prison, but the third, named White Ground had fled to the English. Bienville believed the story, and from then on he treated the Suns with all deference. As a condition of peace, he insisted that the remaining chiefs who had encouraged the murder should be tomahawked.

With that settled, a peace treaty was drawn up. By its terms, the Natchez agreed to help build the new fort and return the stolen property to the French. The peace was ratified and in a few weeks the fort was erected and named Fort Rosalie, in honour of Pontchartrain's wife. Leaving Major Pailloux in charge of the garrison at the new fort, Bienville set out for Mobile. On the return journey, he heard that a Spanish expedition was on its way toward the Red River to found a settlement. To forestall them, he dispatched a sergeant and six soldiers to build a fort at Natchitoches, where St. Denis had set up his little trading post.

Back in Mobile, the successful solution to the Natchez flare-up pleased everyone except Cadillac, who affected to be horrified at the summary executions of the perpetrators, though by all accounts, the Natchez leaders themselves approved of the proceedings, and relations with the French had returned to a cordial footing. Yet Cadillac continued to vent his spleen on Bienville, denouncing his Indian policy to the minister and hinting strongly that he be recalled. Little did he know that he himself was on the way out. While he was grumbling that Louisiana was a "monster" with no form of government, Crozat was blaming him for most of the trouble.

Meanwhile, changes had been taking place in France. In August 1715, after a reign of seventy-two years, Louis XIV died, leaving his 5-year-old great-grandson to succeed him. The following day the king's nephew, the Duc d'Orléans was acclaimed Regent vested with royal authority until King Louis XV came of age. One of the Regent's first acts was to abolish the five or six ministries which reported directly to the king and replace the ministers with councils. Pontchartrain was dismissed and replaced by the Conseil de Marine, headed by King Louis XIV's natural son, the Comte de Toulouse. (Ironically, Pontchartrain was later accused of abusing his position for his personal gain.) In February 1716, Crozat petitioned the new council to recall both Cadillac and Duclos and replace them with more suitable administrators. His candidate for new governor was Jean-Michel de Lépinay, who was accepted all the more readily because he was a protégé of the Comte de Toulouse. Navy commissary Marc-Antoine Hubert replaced

Duclos, and Bienville was appointed commandant of the Wabash (Lower Ohio) region on the Upper Mississippi.

This latest setback was particularly hard on Bienville, who had allowed himself to hope that he was in favor at last. His handling of native affairs was being universally applauded; for some time, Pontchartrain's dispatches were even verging on the complimentary. In a letter to his oldest brother, the Baron de Longueuil, in 1713, he was already predicting that Cadillac's tenure as governor would be short-lived. If he himself succeeded to the governorship, but not otherwise, he told his brother, he would be in a position to marry—and he had a young woman in mind, none other than Cadillac's 20-year-old daughter Madeleine who had a great deal of merit in his eyes. "I would think of asking for her in marriage, if I had your consent and that of my dear sister," the letter continued, "although I should have a great deal of trouble to make up my mind to be the son-in-law of M. de La Mothe on account of all the snarls I see him in with everybody . . . I have not touched upon it yet to the young lady."[3]

One would dearly like to know more about this marriage that never was. On the face of it, the reason is obvious: Cadillac had been retained as governor longer than expected, and of course Bienville had not received the promotion which would have enabled him to support a wife. Yet, oddly enough, he is writing to the Navy Council in 1716 that he had displeased Cadillac by refusing his daughter in marriage. Did Bienville pay some attention to Madeleine and later back off? Or was Cadillac, who had several children to support, overly anxious to get an unmarried daughter off his hands? We do know that there had been some talk of a marriage between Madeleine and Clairambault d'Aigrement when the family was in Detroit, but that arrangement had also fallen through for some reason. Be that as it may, Madeleine accompanied the family to France where she ended her life in a convent. As for the thirty-three-year-old Bienville, his marriage plans were apparently placed on permanent hold.

Meanwhile, as he saw it, his eighteen years of faithful service counted for nothing. Not only had he been passed over for governor yet again, he had been relegated to the distant Wabash, which he took to be a step down from his previous position of commandant of the whole Mississippi Basin. Henceforth he would be a kind of roving Indian agent obliged, as his brother Chateauguay said, to go "wandering in the woods" and among the Indians to make establishments, transporting his goods at his own expense. There was no guarantee that he would even have the dispersal of any presents to the Indians, and no coveted Cross of St. Louis. To add insult to injury,

[3]Letter from Bienville to Longueuil, cited in Grace King, *Jean Baptiste le Moyne, Sieur de Bienville* (New York, 1892), 198-205.

Lépinay and Hubert, and even a Company captain named Sieur d'Artus, received a commission from Crozat on top of their salaries, whereas Bienville was allowed 1 percent on "the merchandise of the country," which was 1 percent of nothing as far as Bienville was concerned.

Actually Bienville's new appointment was not a demotion at all. He was not a Company man, and that alone was enough to disqualify him for the governorship. Nonetheless, the financier respected him for his ability to handle Indian affairs. He was deemed to be the only man who could keep the Indian alliance together in the very important Wabash region, the gateway to the Upper Mississippi Valley, and an area rumored to contain vast deposits of lead and silver.

As it transpired, Lépinay's Louisiana regime was short and inglorious. Perhaps because of his friendship with the Comte de Toulouse, he adopted haughty airs, which antagonized every segment of the population. Even though he had spent a few years in Canada, he had no conception of how to treat the Indians, and in fact he took little or no interest in native matters. By order of the Council, he did build Fort Toulouse on the Alabama River to keep the English in check, but in spite of Bienville's urgings he refused the essential presents to the local chiefs. Very soon Hubert was writing:

> Several [Indian chiefs] are very dissatisfied, and they say among themselves that M. de Lepinay is an old mangy dog whom the Great Chief on the other side of the great lake had sent to this country because he was dying of hunger in his village, and he was an old woman, that he never went out of his house, that he made a big noise but that his words did not go beyond the door of his room.[4]

Hubert went on to recommend that the colony be divided in half with Bienville as one of the commandants because he knew all the Indians and they respected him.

About the time that Hubert was penning his letter, the Prince Regent was in the process of making more changes in Louisiana. Despairing of the Louisiana enterprise, Crozat relinquished his fifteen-year monopoly to the Crown after only five years of doing business, or more accurately of not doing business. The Regent accepted the return of the charter and transferred the monopoly to the newly formed Company of the West headed by the wealthy financier John Law. After less than a year in the colony Lépinay was recalled and nominated governor of Grenada.

The vessel bearing the orders for Lépinay's return from Louisiana brought good news for Bienville. After his many years of service to the

[4]Hubert to the Council, October 26, 1717, *MPA*, 2:249.

colony, he was finally appointed commandant general. With the appointment, his salary was raised to 6,000 *livres* a year and he was awarded the Cross of St. Louis. The territory of Louisiana was also extended to include the country of the Illinois, formerly under the jurisdiction of Canada.

Chapter VI
John Law Makes an Impression

John Law's Company of the West, later known as the Company of the Indies, put Louisiana on the map. For the first time in its history, the colony became the talk of Europe. Hints of mythical gold and the very real land and forest riches of the colony attracted investors to his company, all of them hoping to cash in on a good thing, although they knew little or nothing about Louisiana or its geography. What they were counting on was the financial wizardry of John Law, whose dazzling new "system" was breathing life into France's moribund economy. Not that they understood the system—hardly anybody in France did—but Law was obviously creating wealth where before there had been poverty.

Law's system was based on ideas which would seem elementary today. He saw that money was merely a means of exchange with no absolute intrinsic value; like every commodity its value fluctuated with changes in demand and supply. He also realized that the quantity of money in circulation affected the economy, so when the quantity of precious metals in circulation was too low, as it was in France, commerce declined and recession followed. Placed in this light, paper money, which was cheap and easy to produce, could be substituted for coinage, and as long as the system was managed in such a way as to promote confidence, a bank could print more money than it could redeem at any given time. And that is just what his newly created bank began to do. It issued notes backed only partly by gold, just as modern banks issue currency backed by dependable assets, and thus created credit. So far, so good. The venture was successful, the bills of Law's bank furnished a safe and convenient currency, and whenever presented they were promptly paid in specie. Soon merchants began to undertake new enterprises, interest rates fell, and the economy began to improve. The Prince Regent was so taken with Law's new ideas that he turned Law's private bank into a state institution. The new Royal Bank of France was authorized to issue money, collect taxes, and take over the payment of the national debt. With the profits that he expected from his credit enterprises, Law proposed to develop the Mississippi colony, so when Crozat resigned his privileges, Law's new Company of the West was awarded the monopoly.

By the terms of its contract, the Company of the West was awarded absolute title to Louisiana and its commerce for a period of twenty-five years. In return, Law undertook to develop the colony and send out 6,000 settlers and 3,000 slaves within ten years. To get things off to a good start, the Company made land concessions generally four leagues square to persons or groups who could afford the initial outlay, on condition that the owners undertook to transport 200 settlers each. The trouble was to find the right kind of settlers. An extravagant propaganda machine was set in motion in France and to a lesser extent in Switzerland, Germany, and Holland, all of it depicting Louisiana in the most favorable terms. In the new Utopia, the land was said to produce two crops a year, deer and buffalo with flesh more delicious than the tastiest European meat roamed in profusion everywhere; and the native people were very much attached to the French. It was hoped, wrongly as it transpired, that the glowing picture would have particular appeal for many poor French peasants, worn down as they were with taxes, and with scarcely a piece of meat on the table from one end of the year to the other. As soon as it became obvious that the supply of voluntary emigrants was falling short of expectations, the Company resorted to forced emigration. Although the numbers of undesirables who actually reached the colony were never as high as has been made out, they were enough to cause Bienville endless frustration.

Early in 1718 the first three ships flying the Company flag, featuring the Mississippi and the horn of plenty, flanked by Indians upholding the *fleur-de-lis*, dropped anchor off Dauphin Island. On board was a company of soldiers, several workmen, and about sixty salt smugglers, all of whom had already been recruited by Crozat before he relinquished his grant. To Bienville came the Cross of St. Louis and the all-important royal dispatches raising him to commandant general. To all intents and purposes he was governor of Louisiana, but without the prestige attached to the title—and Bienville would dearly have liked the prestige. In fact, when he had time to study the dispatches, it became clear that his sphere of operations was to be severely restricted. According to the royal edict of September 20, 1717:

> It is our will however that the said Sieur de Bienville may not make any new establishments or change those that are already made, undertake wars against the Indians or make peace or alliances with them except with the consent of the deputies of the said Western Company residing in our said province of Louisiana and in keeping with their decisions which shall be made by a plurality of votes, which he shall be obliged to follow in everything that concerns the welfare and the increase of the commerce and the establishments.[1]

In line with these instructions, a Council of Commerce was to be set up consisting of Bienville in his capacity of commandant general and director general of the Company; Hubert as commissary and director; as well as three more directors and sundry other company officials who arrived later in the year. Chateauguay and Boisbriant represented the military. So,

[1]Commission for Bienville as Commandant General, September 20, 1717, *MPA*, 2:23.

although old hands like Chateauguay and Boisbriant would have their say in the decision-making, there was no doubt that the Company intended to call the shots. As anyone who knew Bienville could have predicted, he was unlikely to sit quietly and allow himself to be overruled by a few bureaucrats and glorified clerks, mere greenhorns as he saw them, who knew nothing about how to handle the Indians, or where to set up a new trading post, or the best location for the proposed new capital. The new directors naturally saw things in quite a different light. Invested with the authority of the Company they had a right to take full part in all deliberations, whereas Bienville felt that the time taken up in arranging meetings and debating routine issues hampered his freedom of action in emergencies. Later, as the council meeting place kept shifting from Dauphin Island to Old Biloxi, to New Biloxi, and finally to New Orleans it was almost impossible to get all the members together. No wonder that decisions were delayed too long, and opinions almost impossible to reconcile about all manner of things, including the site of the capital and the feasibility of sending ships up the Mississippi.

From the beginning, Iberville had envisioned a strong French presence on the Mississippi River, but the deltas and shifting sandbars made the river impassable to large ships. It was to counter the threat of an English thrust into the interior that he established Fort Mississippi, a makeshift post serving more as a symbol of French possession than a military deterrent, which Bienville had to abandon in 1706 because he had no men to guard it. With the arrival of the Company of the West, the axis of settlement was about to shift away from Mobile to the rich Mississippi Valley and efforts were intensified to locate a channel deep enough to allow large vessels to enter the river.

One of the Company's first resolutions (September 1717) was to establish a town "thirty leagues up the river," the town to be named after the Prince Regent, the duc d'Orléans. The following month a cashier and warehouse keeper were appointed for the commercial office to be established at New Orleans. In May 1718, Bienville chose the site on a "fine crescent" on the eastern bank of the river, where the city of New Orleans now stands. No doubt he knew the value of the wide frontage and the easy transportation route from the new site through Bayou St. Jean and Lake Pontchartrain to the coastal centers. Probably he also considered the fact that the difficulty of negotiating ships past English Turn would be enough to deter an enemy fleet from attacking the future capital. Under his direction, 100 men, about 50 of whom were salt smugglers, set about the tedious business of felling trees and clearing canebreaks, and he himself traced out the alignment of the first few streets along the river. To counteract the danger of flooding, he planned to erect levees on the waterfront and to construct a canal linking the river with Lake Pontchartrain. Leaving Major Pailloux in charge of the work crew, he returned to Mobile.

In June 1718 he sent a progress report to France:

> We are working on New Orleans with such diligence as the dearth of workmen will allow. I myself went to the spot to choose the best site. I remained for ten days to hurry on a task which required at least a hundred times the number. All the ground of the site, except the borders which are drowned by floods, is very good and everything will grow there.[2]

Yet strangely, just when the first ground was being cleared, the French directors were still poring over their maps for the best site. Perhaps they had forgotten about their orders to Bienville, or perhaps they did not trust his judgment, or it could be that their maps were at fault. At any rate, in the spring of 1718, they sent out an engineer named Étienne Perrier with instructions to lay out the new town at the confluence of Bayou Manchac and the Mississippi, near the site of the present Plaquemine, Louisiana, or wherever else he deemed fit. Since Perrier died before reaching Louisiana, what decision he might have made is anybody's guess.

For a few years, New Orleans existed only in name. By Bienville's own count, there were only four houses under way in 1719. More of a way station for concessionaires on their journey upriver than a settlement, its future as the capital city hung in the balance. Hardly a notable in the colony had a good word to say for the site. Father Le Maire, an amateur geographer and parish priest of Mobile, advocated a site on Lake Pontchartrain where there was an abundance of fresh water. Hubert, who favored the site initially, later changed his mind in favor of the Natchez country, perhaps because he himself had received a concession there in 1718, and he also encouraged other settlers to bypass New Orleans in favor of the northern post, where the land was less subject to flooding. By 1720 he had eighty slaves and twenty cattle on his new concession in the Natchez area, where he and his wife were experimenting with silk-making. That same year he resigned his directorship of the Company, although he carried on with his duties as commissary. Rightly or wrongly, Bienville became convinced that Hubert also favored the Natchez settlement over New Orleans when it came to allocating provisions. But the most strident opposition to the new town came from Company director Charles Le Gac who battled for years to have the capital moved to Biloxi. Even Bienville himself began to have second thoughts about his "beautiful crescent" after an abnormal rise in the river flooded the site in 1719. Still New Orleans did not die. A few

[2]Bienville to the Council, June 10, 1718, *MPA*, 3:200.

concessionaries, as well as Bienville himself, were granted land in the vicinity and they also took lots in the town.

Meanwhile, Bienville had more pressing business to attend to at the coast. During his absence at New Orleans, Company ships carrying over 600 people had arrived at Dauphin Island. Since the harbor had been choked up with sand by a hurricane in 1717, the newcomers had to be shuttled from the vessels to the island in small craft and then await their turn to be transported up the river to their concessions. The Company had undertaken to provide them with food and transportation to their destination, but the French directors had not reckoned with the fact that there were only a few boats in the colony. Until craft could be found, or built, the newcomers were cooped up on the barren island sometimes as long as three months, without adequate shelter or fresh food. For the most part, the newcomers seem to have been a shiftless lot, quite unable to do much to help themselves. In September Bienville was voicing his frustration to the Company:

> The plan of this great shipment of settlers is incontestably the most advantageous to the colony, but . . . it would have been very advisable to make a more careful selection of the people whom we needed. Doubtless they [the directors] would then have sent us a large number of workmen, especially farmers, carpenters and joiners and they would not have tolerated so many useless mouths in the companies of almost all the holders of the concessions, among whom one scarcely finds one man suitable for the most urgent work. Furthermore, if care had been taken to send us provisions in proportion, in order to support them or at least a number of boats sufficient to supplement the few that seven or eight rather poor house carpenters that we have here have been able to build . . . I should have been relieved of infinite embarrassment.[3]

Among the newcomers were two men whose names are familiar to students of Louisiana history—Bénard de La Harpe and Le Page du Pratz. The former explored the Red River and gave his name to a book which chronicles the early history of the colony. Du Pratz also wrote a history of Louisiana containing a mine of information about the colony and its natural history and particularly about the Natchez Indians, whom he grew to respect and admire during his eight-year stay among them.

While the small colony of no more than 500 souls was trying to cope with the horde of new immigrants, France became embroiled in a war with Spain which was to have repercussions in Louisiana. As wars go, the conflict known as the War of the Quadruple Alliance was a half-hearted affair. The French had no stomach for another war, and the Spaniards, who

[3]Bienville to the Navy Council, September 25, 1718, *MPA*, 3:234-35.

had provoked the conflict in the first place by invading Sardinia, were badly outmatched by an alliance consisting of England, France, Holland, and Austria. All the same, it gave France the excuse it needed to establish new bases along the Gulf of Mexico and drive the Spaniards out of Pensacola, the only good harbor on the gulf.

While war clouds were still looming, the Company of the West ordered Bienville to take possession of St. Joseph's Bay, some fifty leagues east of Dauphin Island. Bienville was less than enthusiastic about the move. The bay was too far removed from the main colony; besides, as he pointed out, the roadstead at Ship Island provided much safer anchorage for French ships. Still an order was an order, especially when it was backed by the Prince Regent, so Bienville dispatched his brother Chateauguay with a detachment of fifty soldiers to take possession of the bay and erect a fort there. Fort Crèvecoeur (Heartbreak Fort) as the new fort was called, lived up to its name. The harbor was unprotected from the winds, the soil around it was poor, and the water unfit to drink. Father Charlevoix who visited the place a few years later saw it as "a flat coast, quite exposed to all the winds that blow, a barren land, a country lost and hid from all the world."[4] In the unhealthy atmosphere, some of the soldiers fell ill or deserted to the Spaniards, who were only too glad to receive them. Two months after it was established, Bienville had the fort burned down and the garrison withdrawn. The whole exercise had been a useless and expensive debacle.

Another foray into territory claimed by Spain was equally unproductive. In August 1718, the Company directors sent Bienville explicit orders to occupy St. Bernard's Bay (Matagorda Bay) on the coast of present-day Texas. France could assert an admittedly dubious claim to the bay. As we have seen, explorer La Salle had stumbled on the bay on his ill-fated voyage to the Mississippi and deluded himself into thinking that it was one of the entrances to the Mississippi. It was not until 1720—and then after more prompting from France—that Bienville saw his way to comply with the Company's request. Captain Béranger, who led the expedition, apparently knew as little about the coast as La Salle did, and the expedition was a failure. The next year another group led by Bénard de La Harpe did reach the place, only to be faced with hostile Indians. With the best intentions in the world, La Harpe, a newcomer to Louisiana who had a lot to learn about how to treat the Indians, lured nine of the natives on board ship and took them to Biloxi in the hope of impressing them with French might—and friendly intentions! "Very embarrassed" by La Harpe's stupidity, Bienville softened up the prisoners with gifts and sent them home. Before the project ever got off the ground it was shelved. As Bienville saw it: "We are not in a

[4]P. F. X. Charlevoix, *Journal of a Voyage to North America*, vol. 2 (London, 1761), 62.

position to maintain a post so distant as that one which would have occupied part of our vessels and our sailors of whom we have a very pressing need. . . ."[5]

No sooner was the War of the Quadruple Alliance officially declared, than the Company jumped at the chance to mount an attack on Pensacola. Two company ships, the *Maréchal de Villars* and the *Comte de Toulouse* carrying soldiers, supplies, and settlers anchored off Dauphin Island in April 1719. Among the passengers was Bienville's brother, Sérigny, bearing orders to besiege and take possession of Pensacola and of everything that belonged to the Spaniards. At a hastily convened meeting of the council of war, it was decided to mount an immediate three-pronged attack on Pensacola. Three frigates led by Sérigny and Company Director Larcebault transported the main force; Bienville's contingent consisting of eighty men in four shallops skirted the coastline; and the third force composed of sixty soldiers and a few hundred Indians led by Chateauguay took the overland route. On May 13, 1719, Bienville's contingent slipped past the harbor entrance and anchored on the western side of Santa Rosa, where there was a small fort. According to some accounts, the French crept up to the fort under cover of darkness, seized the guardhouse, captured the garrison, and donned their uniform. At daybreak when the relief sentries arrived, the disguised Frenchmen struck up a Spanish march and the unsuspecting Spaniards walked straight into the trap. By all account, the rest was child's play; La Page Du Pratz's version has the French stealing into Pensacola and capturing the governor, Matamores de Isla, in his bed! At all events, the fort surrendered without a drop of blood being spilt, amid the governor's protests that France and Spain were not at war at all. Chateauguay was left in command of Pensacola and the 1,400-man Spanish garrison, which would have been sent to France had there been enough provisions for the voyage, were escorted to Havana on the two French ships. On their arrival in Cuba, the French were in for a shock. When Captain Richeburg stepped ashore under a flag of truce to present the terms of capitulation, the irate governor, Gregorio Guazo Calderon, refused to honor the agreement signed in Pensacola that neither side would attack the other for one week after the departure of the vessels. Instead, Richeburg and all his men were arrested and the two French ships seized.

With two French ships and lots of troops at their disposal, the Spaniards were determined to counterattack. On August 7, a Spanish flotilla led by the *Maréchal de Villars* flying the *fleur-de-lis* entered Pensacola Bay. It was now the French turn to be surprised. Chateauguay managed to get word out to Bienville, who rushed off to his assistance

[5]Bienville to the Navy Council December 15, 1721, *MPA*, 3:313-14.

accompanied by Sérigny and their nephew, Gilles-Augustin Payen de Noyan, and a party of Indians. It was too late. The Spanish flag was already flying over Pensacola, while the strains of Spanish guitars pealed out in victory. Chateauguay's force of 250 men—mainly "a band of deserters, smugglers and scoundrels who are always ready not only to abandon you but also to turn against you" according to Bienville—had deserted in droves to the superior force. The result was a foregone conclusion. After three days of waiting for reinforcements that never came, Chateauguay surrendered. A dispirited letter rushed off by Chateauguay to Bienville on August 9 tells the story, and incidentally illustrates the close ties between the Le Moyne brothers:

> I am writing to you very hastily, my dear brother, as I go on board ship. You will doubtless learn before receiving my letter that we have surrendered with the most advantageous terms that we could make since they had 1600 men in twelve vessels. We are now being put on a boat to go to Havana and from there to Spain. You must think, my dear brother, in what sorrow I must be. The Spaniards expect to drive out the entire French colony. They are expecting from day to day four ships of sixty cannons from Vera Cruz. . . . Neither the time nor the sorrow that I feel permit me to write you at greater length. Mr. Lescarbeault does not have time to write to you, nor I to my brother Sérigny. Be sure to embrace him for me. . . .[6]

Chateauguay's report of an impending attack on the colony was also confirmed by young Payen de Noyan who was allowed into Pensacola under a flag of truce. The governor received him kindly, even to the extent of providing him with provisions for the return journey, still insisting that there was no war on! De Noyan wrote to Bienville saying that the governor really wanted to be friends with the French. However, the flagship commander had quite a different story. He informed De Noyan that he wished to take Dauphin Island and Mobile and even go as far as into the Mississippi.

Thus forewarned, Sérigny set out for Dauphin Island, while Bienville doubled back to Mobile to muster reinforcements. In this emergency, Bienville counted on the support of his Indian allies, and he was not disappointed. Early in August, Juchereau de St. Denis brought a contingent of Pascagoula Indians to the island; almost simultaneously François Trudeau arrived with another native contingent and a force of Canadians noted for their marksmanship. On their way to the battlefront, a third

[6]Copy of the letter of Chateauguay written to Bienville from Pensacola August 9, 1719, *MPA*, 3:251-52.

group, led by Sr. de Villainville, ambushed and routed a party of Spanish looters and deserters from Chateauguay's garrison.

On the morning of August 13, a Spanish flotilla approached Dauphin Island. The following day a messenger brought a high-handed letter from Captain Mandieta, leader of the Spanish fleet, ordering Sérigny to surrender, or see everyone, including Chateauguay, put to the sword. Sérigny, of course, refused; and the Indians in his entourage, dressed in their feathers and warpaint scared the messenger half to death as they "let it be known by their countenance that they were only awaiting permission to scalp this officer."

The French position was by no means enviable. Apart from the Indians, Sérigny had only 160 soldiers, part of whom were said to be much more to be feared than the enemies themselves. The Spanish squadron began by cannonading the *Philippe*, a French ship loaded with merchandise, but they were repulsed without doing much damage to the vessel. Two attempts at landing were no more successful against the combined fire of the Canadians and the Indians. After twelve days of intermittent exchanges of fire, the Spaniards departed, much to the surprise of the French who considered the departure a ruse. Sérigny's worst fears seemed to be confirmed a few days later when five ships appeared on the horizon, four flying the Spanish flag. Was this the Spanish fleet from Vera Cruz that Chateauguay had mentioned in his letter to Bienville? As the ships neared the shore, they hoisted the *fleur-de-lis*; this was no Spanish flotilla but a French squadron under the command of Commodore Danos de Champmeslin.

The arrival of the vessels provided an excellent opportunity to recapture Pensacola before help arrived from Vera Cruz. In a week the arrangements were completed. Bienville set off in a launch with 100 soldiers to join 400 Indians who were waiting for him by the Perdido River; and Champmeslin, Sérigny, and Company Director Villardeau sailed off with the fleet. On the night of September 16, Champmeslin could make out the fires of Bienville's camp about a league from Pensacola. Next morning after giving the signal to Champmeslin, Bienville led his Canadian and Indian fighters on the attack, and Champmeslin's fleet slipped into the harbor. Hopelessly outnumbered and short of ammunition, the Spaniards shortly surrendered. In the encounter, the French had only six casualties. The Spaniards lost sixty men together with 1,200 prisoners, forty-seven of whom were French deserters.

After the departure of the Spaniards, the French retained Pensacola as a look-out post, and the port remained in French hands until the end of the war.

In the long run, all the alarums and excursions attending the Pensacola affair ended in futility, and worse than futility. The French gained nothing from the exercise, and many settlers were marooned on Dauphin Island for several months using up their provisions when they could have been transported to their concessions. As usual, events in Europe had had their repercussions in Louisiana. The War of the Quadruple Alliance was stuttering to a close in the spring of 1720, and in his eagerness to get peace negotiations over and done with, the Prince Regent sacrificed Pensacola. In November 1722, the post was formally handed back to the Spaniards and the old borrowing and bartering between Pensacola and Mobile were resumed as before.

Meanwhile the French and the Spaniards jockeyed for position in the no-man's territory of East Texas which La Salle had claimed for France in the mistaken belief that the area was in the Mississippi drainage system. A few miles north of Matagorda Bay tucked away in a secluded spot by the banks of the Lavaca River, the explorer had founded his ill-fated colony, which he named Fort-St.-Louis. No fewer than four Spanish expeditions left Vera Cruz to destroy Fort-St.-Louis. The trouble was to find it. Five years went by before the Spanish explorer, Alonso de Leon, found the shattered ruins of the colony and a handful of wretched survivors, who presented no threat to anyone. Nonetheless, as a way of preventing further French intrusion into the area, the Spaniards established a permanent mission settlement on the Trinity River. Epidemics and the threat of hostile Indians drove the priests away in 1693, though Spain still considered the area an extension of New Mexico.

There the matter remained until Iberville came to Louisiana. It will be remembered that Bienville explored the Red River across the entire breadth of Louisiana back in 1701 in search of La Salle's colony and to find out all he could about the Mexican mines. Before the cold weather and swollen rivers forced him and his party to turn back, he learned something about the terrain and he established good relations with several Indian tribes along the river. One of his companions on the journey was Juchereau de St. Denis. It was mainly because of his high standing among the Caddoan tribes west of the Mississippi that Cadillac had chosen Saint Denis to lead the trading expedition to the Mexican outposts on the Red River and in East Texas. As we have seen, the trading venture was a failure, but of it came the foundation of the little trading post at Natchitoches, on an island in the Red River. Spain moved quickly against this new threat of French encroachment, but Bienville was quicker. At wind of the projected Spanish expedition, Bienville sent a small force to establish a military fort at Natchitoches in 1716. Less than two weeks later the Spaniards set up a mission post at San Miguel de Linares de los Adais about twenty miles away, to keep an eye on their aggressive neighbors. Apparently, Bienville received assurances from the missionary in charge that he was only coming to conduct his mission and preach the gospel. In spite of this verbal assurance, the Spaniards shortly erected a military post in the area.

The war provided Bienville with a good opportunity to rid Natchitoches of its pesky neighbors. An order was rushed out to Corporal Blondel, who commanded in the absence of St. Denis, to expel the missionaries from Los Adais, on the grounds that the fort was on French territory. Evidently the fathers thought discretion was the better part of valor, for they beat a hasty retreat before Blondel's arrival.

To the Spaniards, of course, this was just one more example of French aggression. A few months earlier, Bénard de La Harpe had had the temerity to establish himself on the great bend of the Red River near the present city of Texarkana. La Harpe had been granted a concession in the contested territory, with orders to make alliances with the important Caddoan confederacy, to open trade with the Spaniards, and to explore the Red River to its source. On his arrival at his post, La Harpe called a massive meeting of the tribes, loaded them with gifts and promised to supply them with all their needs. He even initiated cordial relations with Father Marsillo, the missionary in charge of the Spanish missions in East Texas, who was quite willing to deal with anyone, French or Spaniard, if it would help him to maintain his mission. La Harpe very soon learned that the civil authority, in the person of the viceroy of Texas, Don Martin de Alarcon, took a different view of the proceedings. "It must be," he wrote to La Harpe, "that your governor [Bienville] does not know that the post which you occupy belongs to my government . . . I advise you to make this known to M. de Bienville or you will oblige me to force you to abandon the lands on which the French have no right to settle."[7] La Harpe called the governor's bluff, telling him to come and find out for himself how well the post was defended. As La Harpe suspected, Alarcon was too weak to avail himself of the offer. Having nothing to fear from the Spaniards, he continued his way all across the grasslands of eastern Oklahoma as far as the Canadian River, after which he faced homewards.[8]

Meanwhile not everyone was happy to hear that the Spaniards had been ousted from their post at Los Adais. La Harpe did not like it because their departure would cut into the trade that he expected to do with them at his new post; St. Denis, the Natchitoches post commander, did not like it for the same reason, and the Company was more interested in profits than in getting embroiled in another armed struggle. Consequently, Blondel was

[7]*The Historical Journal of the Establishment of the French in Louisiana* [attributed to Bénard de La Harpe]. Edited and translated by Glenn Conrad (Lafayette, La., 1968), 136-37.

[8]Ibid., 138-39.

forced to write a humble apology to the Spanish priests, asking them to return. The following year a Spanish force of about 500 men arrived back at Los Adais and rebuilt the fort. Bienville wrote a strongly worded letter to the Spanish commandant denouncing the "usurpers," but that was as far as he was able to go.

After all the commotion, not much was changed on the Red River. Even while maintaining cordial relations on a day-to-day basis, the Spaniards at Los Adais and the French at Natchitoches still eyed each other a bit suspiciously across the river, and St. Denis continued with his discreet smuggling, while keeping all his Indian neighbors at peace with the French. La Harpe's expeditions gained no new territory for Louisiana, although they did open up trade with the tribes along the Red River and made friends of three important nations—the Caddos, the Wichitas and the Comanches.

Meanwhile to the north plans were afoot to push into the Missouri Valley, make alliances with the local tribes and perhaps discover a route to Santa Fe. No region was more inviting than this fertile valley teeming with wild game and reportedly rich in iron and silver. For a long time, Bienville had itched to get a foothold in the valley; as far back as 1707 he had dispatched a man called Darrac and two companions to make alliances with the Indians and trade for buffalo hides. The man he now chose to venture into the valley to pacify the warring tribes and make friends and customers for the Company of the West was Claude-Charles du Tisné, an audacious adventurer, much admired by the Indians for his courage, but less popular with the clergy and other officials for his dissolute ways. Starting from the Illinois post, Du Tisné and his party pushed up the Missouri River as far as the present Kansas City, but the Missouri Indians would not allow him to continue further, probably fearing that he would supply their enemies with guns. Turning southward to the mouth of the Osage River, he visited the Osages and the Pawnees in turn. Both tribes welcomed him heartily but neither wished him to visit the other in case their enemies would destroy them. Nothing could induce the Pawnees to let him go forward to the Padoucas (Apaches) who were feared by the other tribes, even without the weapons that Du Tisné might give them. Seeing that the Pawnees were becoming surly when he pressed the point, he reluctantly headed for the Illinois post.

In a letter to Bienville in 1719, he reported that all the tribes were eager for trade goods. As for the route to Santa Fe, it would be possible only if the French could pacify the Comanches, which would be a costly business.

The Company turned the task of winning over the hostile tribes to Étienne Véniard de Bourgmond, a man cast from very much the same mold as Du Tisné. A marine officer turned *coureur de bois*, Bourgmond had spent four years voyaging up and down the Missouri, all along, keeping Bienville abreast of his travels, and in 1719 he came to the colony and took part in the attack on Pensacola. Bienville considered him to be the only man who could make peace between the Padoucas and all the other tribes friendly to the French and recommended him for the Cross of St. Louis. Shortly thereafter, Bourgmond sailed for France to present Bienville's ideas about the Missouri territory to the duc d'Orléans. By the time he arrived in Paris, Law's company had collapsed. Because of the confusion surrounding the bankruptcy it was not until 1722 that the newly re-vamped Company of the Indies handed him his commission to establish a post on the Missouri River and put an end to the Padouca wars. As part of the agreement he undertook to bring some important chiefs to France, in order to impress them with the might and glory of the country and perhaps revive interest in Louisiana.

On his return to the colony, he was chagrined to discover that Bienville and most of the other officials had turned against the project. Short of boats, provisions, and men, Louisiana could ill afford to supply and maintain the existing posts, let alone finance a new venture. Nevertheless, Bourgmond pressed on. After many vexations and near-mutinies he established Fort d'Orléans about 270 miles from the mouth of the Missouri, where he rallied together the Otos, the Osages, the Pawnees, the Iowas, and the Kansas tribes. Even the Padoucas eventually agreed to a treaty.

Bourgmond and his six-person delegation returned to France on the *Gironde*. Everywhere the Indians went they created a sensation. The people of Paris flocked to see them and the ladies and gentlemen of the court showered them with attention and gifts. They were also received by the Directors of the Company of the Indies and later presented to the young King Louis XV himself.

Bourgmond himself fared less successfully. Ill and burdened with debts which the Company refused to pay, he remained in France in order to press for reimbursement of all the expenses he had incurred. All of the Indians except one who died en route returned to Louisiana without him. As for Fort d'Orléans, it was abandoned a few years later.

Perhaps the only benefit that resulted from the expedition was the treaty with the Padoucas. With the bad blood that existed between the Fox Indians and the Illinois, the French settlement in that region would scarcely have survived if the warlike Padoucas had also gone on the attack.

Chapter VII
An Influx of Settlers

Meanwhile in France, John Law was enjoying a huge success. Merchants who were originally sceptical of his newfangled ideas about credit and paper money began borrowing and depositing money, secure in the knowledge that the currency was safe and stable. What was more, they no longer needed to carry around sacks of coins from place to place, and the new credit system enabled them to do business on a scale ten times the value of their own investment. The Prince Regent was as dazzled as everyone else with the financial miracle. So in 1719, a royal edict allowed Law to merge the Company of the West with the East India Company and the Company of China. The new company under the name of the Company of the Indies virtually controlled France's world trade. Hordes of investors from Princes of the Blood to lackeys began buying shares in the Company, convinced that Law was a financial wizard who could do no wrong.

The euphoria spurred more interest in Louisiana, and new investors began to apply for land concessions. In their capacities as director general and director respectively, Bienville and Hubert also allotted themselves large tracts. Bienville received two parcels in the vicinity of New Orleans, one running roughly from the present Bienville St. to Southport, and the other on the opposite side of the river in the area known as Algiers; and Hubert's concession (which he later exchanged for a four-square-mile parcel in Natchez country) extended from the eastern side of Point St. Antoine to Lake Pontchartrain. Several syndicates also came into being in France, some headed by rich and prominent people who obtained extensive concessions in the colony. Among the noteworthy investors were wealthy financier Paris Duverney, the Comte de Belle Isle, and Claude Le Blanc, the minister of war; and Law allotted himself a vast *seigneurie* on the Arkansas River and another at English Turn. Of course these men had no intention of ever going to Louisiana. They hired overseers to manage their concessions and undertook to send out settlers to work the land. Law himself recruited hundreds of Germans for his two concessions.

Nonetheless, the supply of settlers willing to emigrate to the colony fell short of expectations, so the Company stepped up its program of forced emigration. Prisons and workhouses were combed for able-bodied men and women, and groups of armed thugs, nicknamed the "*bandoliers* of Louisiana" were hired to round up vagabonds, tramps, and domestic servants out of work for more than four days. Quite frequently the *bandoliers* went far beyond the bounds of their authority and arrested innocent people merely going about their business. A poor provincial on a visit to Paris, or a man who had imbibed too freely could find himself arrested and dragged in chains to L'Orient to await shipment to Louisiana. After a string of complaints, the *bandoliers* were disbanded, and a royal edict forbade any more forced deportation. But the damage was done. Louisiana had acquired the reputation of a penal colony, a reputation it took a long time to live down. In fact, only about 1,300 undesirables actually reached the colony and many of them took to the woods or went to an early grave.

Beginning in 1720, French vessels usually anchored off Ship Island. From there the passengers were transported to an improvised campsite at Biloxi, the site of the former Fort Maurepas. The place was chosen by a majority vote of the council over the objections of Bienville who had first-hand knowledge of that wretched place, where so many people had perished in the long, hot summer of 1700. A worse place could hardly have been found—cramped, without good drinking water and surrounded by mosquito-ridden swamps. The five-league boat trip through the shallow waters and shifting sands separating Ship Island from the mainland was slow and laborious. In some cases, boats capsized, people were cast adrift, and even drowned. The future of Louisiana, and Bienville's future as well, might have been far different if the idea of a coastal settlement had been abandoned, and incoming vessels, at least those of lower tonnage, had been sent up the river.

The decision not to send any ships up the Mississippi was the result of bad luck, bad judgment, and inhospitable geography. There were those who believed that the river could never be made navigable. In 1719, Hubert was writing that the sandbars and shifting currents made river access virtually impossible, and Le Gac did everything in his powers to discourage the idea. Bienville, who probably knew the river better than anyone, was not so pessimistic. After sounding the bar in 1718, he informed the Company:

> In the absolute necessity that we are in of having a commodious and safe port without which the colony will never be able to be established solidly, it appears to me that if we could dredge this bar with machines we could make one in this place as advantageous as could be wished. . . .[1]

That same year the engineer Perrier was sent to the colony with instructions to try to shift the bar, but, as we know, he died on the voyage and the project died with him. The war with Spain put any further plans for dredging on hold. The problem could have been resolved with the arrival of the corps of engineers in December 1720. In fact, Chief Engineer Leblond de La Tour, with Bienville's support, but opposed by Le Gac, was in favor

[1]Bienville to the Navy Council, June 12, 1718, *MPA*, 3:229.

of sending all the smaller vessels upriver. Several months passed before engineer Adrien de Pauger had a chance to thoroughly sound the mouth of the river. Miracle of miracles, he found that the forces of nature had cleared and deepened the main channel. On March 4, 1722, Bienville was writing to the Regent: "You will see by the letter and the map that we are assured of a port for vessels of the third class . . . and that the bar at the entrance will easily be removed."[2] With a little dredging, the Mississippi was soon open to all vessels. But the delay was fatal.

At a council meeting in December 1720, it had been decided to erect another littoral site, usually called New Biloxi, where the present city of Biloxi now stands. The new site was better, but not much better, than the old one. It is true that the area was higher and more spacious, but incoming ships still had to dock four leagues from the shore. Apparently, Bienville was opposed to the move, on the grounds that it would be necessary to relocate yet again some time in the future, but he was outvoted. The chief engineer, Leblond de La Tour, supervised the move and planned the new Saint-Louis de Biloxi. Until the spring of 1722 New Biloxi became the seat of the government and the landing place for all new immigrants, except for the slaves and some of the poorer immigrants who remained at Old Biloxi.

In the meantime, back in France John Law's wonderful "system" had collapsed. As his bank's paper money had become more popular, the value of the shares skyrocketed. The person who bought a share in October 1719, for example, and sold it a month later made a profit of 1000 percent on his investment. Then the inevitable happened—people began to sell their shares. This of course saddled the bank with enormous debts, which it was unable to meet. As the rush of panic selling continued, the slide downhill to financial catastrophe was swift and sure. The Regent's efforts to sustain the tottering credit of the bank only succeeded in making matters worse. On October 10, 1720, the bank closed its doors, and Law was forced to flee the country in disgrace.

Communications at the time being what they were, the news did not reach Louisiana until the following June. Meanwhile, hundreds of immigrants were still arriving in Biloxi.

Thus began one of the great tragedies of history. On reaching Louisiana after a long voyage, confined to fetid cabins or huddled together on deck exposed to the winds, rain and heat, many of the emigrants were already weak and ill when they reached the colony. What faced them in their new home was misery and confusion. Scattered all around Biloxi were soldiers, sailors, hired laborers, slaves, salt smugglers, concessionaries, and

[2]Bienville to the Navy Council, March 4, 1722, *MPA*, 3:315.

forced immigrants, all awaiting boats to carry them up the river. Food shortages were acute. In the beginning some of the wealthier concessionaries with a little to spare donated food to the less fortunate. When they refused to help out any further, Bienville was obliged to order them to contribute. All this naturally upset the concessionaries, who blamed the authorities in Louisiana for their misfortunes and heaped insults on the colonial company directors. Still Bienville's personal authority was sufficient to deter any attacks on him.

The main foods available were maize and rice, and even maize was scare because of a bad crop year in 1720. Newcomers disliked the maize, and a constant diet of rice was hardly more palatable. Of course the coastal waters abounded with fish, but the trouble was to catch the fish without the necessary equipment. When caught they had to be boiled like everything else, because of a lack of other cooking facilities. Wild game was scarce in the vicinity of Biloxi; and what the Indians managed to supply had to be hauled a long way and eaten on the spot. For the hundreds of hungry people, the supply of poultry, dairy products and eggs that the older inhabitants could provide was a mere drop in the bucket, and the provisions which arrived from France from time to time were never enough to go around. What everyone longed for was French bread, which had to be rationed to a pound a day and eventually to half that amount.

The unsanitary conditions, probably worsened by an infestation of rats, rapidly spread disease and death. One concession lost almost half of its 200 workers in the space of a few days. In late 1721, Leblond de La Tour estimated that 500 people had died in Biloxi in the previous six months. Debilitated by the climate and demoralized by the dreadful conditions, the survivors sank into despair, longing for nothing but to return to France. Since the last thing the French government wanted was an exodus of people to spread the word about the miseries of Louisiana, Bienville was ordered not to allow anyone to leave.

The most pitiful people were the slaves. Those who survived the hunger, thirst, and disease on the fetid slave ships were often worn out with fever by the time they reached the settlement. With so many mouths to feed in Biloxi, the slaves barely got enough food to keep body and soul together, and what they got was of the poorest quality.

Shipments of German immigrants originally slated to work on John Law's Arkansas concession were hardly better off. Of the 4,000 hopeful immigrants, hundreds perished of disease and hunger at French ports while awaiting transport to Louisiana. On the voyage across the ocean, an epidemic turned the vessels into pest ships. To crown their misfortune, the last remnants of the sorry contingent discovered on their arrival that they could no longer count on the Company's previous assurances to help them out until the first crop came in; Law had already fled, leaving them to fend for themselves. After many hardships, these worthy people gave up and petitioned to be sent back to Europe. Fortunately for Louisiana, Bienville persuaded them to settle on the west bank of the Mississippi about twenty-five miles from New Orleans in the place which became known as the German Coast. In a few short years their carefully cultivated farms and gardens would be supplying New Orleans with an abundance of fresh food.

When word of the death and misery at Biloxi reached the mother country, Louisiana's reputation, bad enough as it was already, fell even lower; it would be a long time to come before people could be persuaded to go to the colony of their own free will. Just how many immigrants managed to survive the hardships on land and on sea is difficult to estimate, so conflicting are the statistics. One overview states that 7,020 Europeans and 600 slaves were sent to the colony between 1717 and 1721, and of those 2,000 died or returned to France. Another estimate puts the net population gain at 5,020, after figuring in deaths of 1,300 at Biloxi. Taking subsequent losses, deaths and departures into account, the total gain in population was probably about 3,500 persons.

French officials held Bienville to blame for the confusion and the immense loss of human life. Apparently it did not occur to them—or they were unwilling to admit—that the grandiose scheme had been too hasty and too poorly planned. A poor colony with a few hundred inhabitants, no sure harbor, and no infrastructure could not possibly have housed and fed the hordes of humanity dumped on its shores all at once. In the dying months of the Law regime, the Prince Regent, who was probably feeling the heat himself for his earlier endorsement of the financier's system, delivered a sharp dressing down to Bienville. Instead of receiving the rank of brigadier and the Order of Commander of St. Louis, both of which had already been promised to him, Bienville was told that the graces of the king were only given for services performed and therefore Bienville must wait until he had earned them.

Cut to the quick by the Regent's strictures, Bienville presented himself as a long-suffering man, battling against endless obstacles and provocations:

> I have the honour to inform the Council that this colony is hampered in its establishment by the lack of method that has been adopted in France in sending many people and few supplies and merchandise, and by the confusion and lack of method that has always prevailed. . . . I have taken all sorts of pains and undergone all sorts of hardships for its advantage in order to merit the protection of the directors who are invested with powers which I have had to submit to with mortification, for they have contributed no little to the disorders

> that have occurred, since I have not been free to put into execution the advantageous plans I had devised.[3]

All things considered, he had good reason to feel humiliated by the appointment of a new director Michel-Léon Duvergier, who arrived in Louisiana in July 1722. The new *Directeur-Ordonnateur*, who had the same salary as Bienville, had far more authority than his predecessor, Marc-Antoine Hubert, who had returned to France earlier in the year. As well as presiding over the Council of Commerce, Duvergier had the power to requisition troops, oversee the fortifications, and approve or veto civil and military expenses. Compared to him Bienville had very little freedom of action. He would still preside over the Council of War, which handled Indian policy and military matters, where no doubt his opinion would carry considerable weight. Nonetheless, he had just one vote like everyone else on the council.

The new arrangement was entrusting a great deal of authority to a man who knew nothing at all about Louisiana and apparently cared still less about it. In fact, when he heard about the general disorder in the colony during a stop-off in Saint Domingue, Duvergier immediately wrote to France for his recall "because of his health." On his arrival he complained about everything—the poverty of the colony, the mediocre quality of the Company directors, and his own poor health. Other than attending a few council meetings and dismissing a few officers who were not to his liking, he did little or nothing worthy of attention. When word of Law's defection spread, disgruntled settlers vented their spleen on him and the other Company director, Sr. Delorme. Disgusted with everything, he returned to France after only eight months at his post. Nobody missed him in Louisiana, and apparently he was arrested on his return to France for leaving the colony without permission.

In the meantime, the Regent had appointed a board of commissioners to handle the bankruptcy and reorganization of the Company of the Indies. After several months of deliberation, the commissioners issued an interim report outlining new policies and directives aimed at improving the colony's administrative structure and putting its financial house in order.

For a start, the vast territory was divided into nine military districts—New Orleans, Biloxi, Mobile, the Alabama, the Natchez, the Yazoos, the Natchitoches, the Arkansas, and the Illinois, each with its own commandant and a judge to settle the usual minor disputes. In keeping with their intention to wring some return from the Louisiana investment, the commissioners placed business matters front and center. The mark-up to be

[3]Bienville to the Navy Council, July 20, 1721, *MPA*, 3:304-5.

charged for French merchandise; the quality and price of tobacco, rice, and other items sold to the Company; the cost of a Company slave, and the punishment for unpaid debts—all these and more were spelled out in detail with appropriate warnings for non-compliance. Tucked in with regulations about the price of brandy and the way to pack tobacco was an admonition for the settlers to be more regular in fulfilling their duties as Christians. (As yet there were only one or two poor churches in the whole colony.)

It fell to the Louisiana council to put the new regulations into effect. At the risk of offending the French commissioners, the council occasionally modified decrees which the general population considered entirely too harsh. They gave consideration to those who were unable to pay for slaves within the required time, and eased prices a little in order to "prevent a revolution." And in spite of an order from the commissioners not to permit anyone whomsoever to return to France on any pretext, the council allowed the chronically ill and widows burdened with families to leave the colony, for the simple reason that there was not enough medicine or food to go around.

No doubt Bienville would have liked to rid the colony of undesirables as well. As already noted, Louisiana had received more than its fair share of rogues and drifters during the Law regime. Even though many of them eventually vanished from the scene, there were still enough of these people in the major settlements to cause disturbances. In addition, there were several young "libertines" from respectable French families sent to Louisiana to get them out of the way. Freed from the social restraints of family and kin, these ne'er-do-wells carried on with their dissolute behavior in the new country. They scandalized their respectable neighbors by consorting with women of easy virtue, both French and Indian, and their drinking, gambling, and carousing continued far into the night, even on Sundays and church holidays. In an effort to curb the gambling, the Council imposed fines for Sunday opening, outlawed certain games of chance, and declared IOUs surpassing 100 *livres* to be null and void. By all accounts, the regulations merely drove the abuses underground.

What Louisiana conspicuously lacked was the moderating effect of the church. At the time, there were only two or three priests in the colony, except for the few chaplains brought out by owners of large concessions, and these could have little or no influence on the general population. As Bienville had learned from his experiences in Canada, priests drew well-defined lines between what their parishioners could and could not do, which at least had the effect of preserving public decency. The colorful liturgy of the church also brought a certain dignity into the rough lives of the settlers and served as a link to the past. Denied the solace of the familiar rituals and cut off forever from the Old World, the newcomers must have felt adrift in the strange new land.

Everything disheartened them. There was never enough food, and the food that was available took some getting used to. One of the first regulations laid down by the commissioners made it clear that flour would no longer be distributed to anyone except soldiers and Company workmen unless paid for in the "products of the country." When the Louisiana Council tried to put the edict into effect, it encountered a barrage of opposition. It was hard enough for the settlers to become accustomed to bread made from rice and corn meal, even worse they had no mills to grind the grain. Provisions from France were extraordinarily dear because of the high inflation in the mother country and the Louisiana price mark-up, ranging from 50 percent in the coastal centers to 100 percent in the Illinois country. Some shady dealings pushed prices even higher. Sailors and others stole goods from Company ships, Company clerks held back goods and later sold them for what the traffic would bear, and settlers with produce to sell kept hiking their prices far above the prescribed rate.

This widespread profiteering, or "usury" as Bienville called it, was especially hard on the poor and those on fixed incomes such as the soldiers. Very likely the bad conditions were largely responsible for a number of desertions and even mutinies. In July 1722, a Swiss company on its way to New Orleans commandeered a freighter and forced the captain to take the soldiers to Havana. After being refused entrance to Cuba, the men ended up settling in Carolina. The garrison at Fort Toulouse mutinied, killed their captain, Marchand de Courcelles, and made off for Carolina as well, before being apprehended. Prisoners carried off pirogues laden with food, and ex-convicts pillaged stores at the Law concession. Otherwise decent people were driven to crime to survive. Historian Father Charlevoix, who was visiting the colony at the time, relates:

> One Duclos, commanding a coaster with a very rich cargo, was met by a party of these deserters, who merely took from him some provisions and liquors, without touching his merchandise. On his expressing his surprise, they replied that they were not robbers but decent men whom necessity forced to seek life in other nations, since their own let them perish of hunger.[4]

Innumerable edicts were enacted to regulate the price of food and beverages, but no matter what the regulation the prices continued to rise. The more unscrupulous elements took to killing their neighbors' cattle, an easy thing to do in a wide open place like Louisiana. To curb what must have been a fairly widespread practice, a soldier was given his discharge and

[4]F. X. Charlevoix, *History and General Description of New France*. Translated with notes by J. G. Shea, 6 (1866-72): 69.

a convict his release on reporting such a theft. The council also addressed itself to other issues of morality and good order. Regulations were put in place to register births, marriages, and deaths, and to ensure that the property of the deceased was sealed so that an inventory could be made for the heirs. The same regulation was also a means of checking on bigamous or irregular relationships. The council also turned its attention to abuses in the medical profession. With all the illnesses that were rife in the colony, quacks must have been having a field day, because a decree went out that anyone found practicing without a license was liable to criminal prosecution.

The arrival of the engineers helped push forward one of Bienville's happiest plans, the layout of New Orleans. Although the Company's main business office was in the new town, several people were still not happy with the site. Apparently in two minds about the place, the French directors had empowered Chief Engineer Leblond de La Tour to examine Bienville's site and change it if he saw fit. Adrien de Pauger, the engineer entrusted with the task, was more impressed with English Turn at first, but on further consideration he came around to Bienville's way of thinking about the capital's strategic position:

> You have been told that because New Orleans is above English Turn that ships require a considerable amount of time to get there from the mouth of the river and that if the city were below they would get there in twenty four hours with a favourable wind. I used to agree with that argument, but experience has made me see that precisely the contrary is true. . . . If an enemy vessel with a good wind behind it could get past the batteries at the mouth of the Mississippi it could push on to New Orleans and burn the storehouses if it were not stopped by the English Turn.[5]

In March 1721, Pauger arrived at the site to trace out the ground plan. What greeted his eyes was a Company storehouse together with a few ramshackle homes scattered here and there among the trees and canebreaks. He had to fight Delorme and Company clerk Froebel every inch of the way in order to get workmen to clear the ground and help with the layout. Finally Sieur de Pailloux, major general of the colony and a loyal Bienville supporter, put some of his soldiers to work and the pace picked up. In a few weeks enough ground was cleared to lay out the first rows of blocks fronting the river, although it would be ten years before Leblond de La Tour's map of January 1723 would be close to the reality.

[5]Pauger to Directors, May 29, 1724. *Archives de Colonies*, series C13A, 10, 53.

Highly colored reports of the new capital carrying the illustrious name of the Prince Regent began to appear in French newspapers. However, when Father Charlevoix passed through the place in January 1722, this is what he saw:

> This is the first city which one of the greatest rivers in the world has seen erected on its banks. If the eight hundred fine houses and the five parishes which the *Mercure* [a French newspaper] bestowed upon it two years ago are at present reduced to a hundred huts, placed in no very good order; to a large warehouse built of timber; to two or three houses which would be no ornament to a village in France; to one half of a sorry warehouse formerly set apart for divine service . . . what pleasure can it give, on the other hand to see this future capital of an immense and beautiful country . . . this wild and desert place almost entirely covered over shall one day, and perhaps that day is not far off, become the capital of a large and rich colony.[6]

In June 1722, Bienville moved his residence to New Orleans, which henceforth was the capital in fact as well as in name. Like many things in Louisiana, New Orleans had its share of bad luck. There were times when ships almost ran aground on their way to the capital. Then came the great hurricane of September 1722, which flooded the town and levelled several houses. Nevertheless, New Orleans survived everything and grew into the great city predicted by Charlevoix.

With the removal of the capital to New Orleans, Mobile lost several inhabitants, although it continued to be of strategic importance as the hub of the fur trade and the center of Indian diplomacy. Chateauguay, the commandant at the newly named Fort Condé at Mobile and a man highly respected by the Indians, kept a watchful eye on potential trouble spots. He moved quickly to alert his brother to the possible defection of the Apalachees. These Indians who had left their old homelands to settle near Mobile in 1704 had been loyal to the French for years, perhaps too loyal for their own good. Since they were Christians, and even adopted French dress and French customs, their fidelity had been taken for granted. But fidelity had its limits. Seeing that they had been left without a priest since the departure of the ailing Father Huvé, they came to Chateauguay in a body threatening to go back to Pensacola unless they got a pastor. The ultimatum brought speedier results than the natives had dared to hope for. Two Carmelite priests had just arrived in the colony and one of them was promptly sent to the Apalachee mission.

The Choctaws used blackmail of a different kind in order to wrest better trade deals from their old allies: the French would have to find a way to

[6] F. X. Charlevoix, *Journal*, 2:275-76.

deliver cheaper and more abundant trade goods closer to their villages or the natives would consider taking advantage of tempting offers from the Carolinians. During the upheavals of the Law years, the Choctaws had been somewhat neglected. His hands full trying to cope with streams of immigrants, and with a Council of War to report to, Bienville had been unable to take matters into his own hands when the occasion demanded. Besides, some Company officials felt that the Choctaws were far too demanding. To be sure, the Choctaws knew how to use the English overtures as leverage—they would not have been human if they did not—but they were no fair-weather friends. During the war with Spain, they had neglected their crops and left their wives and families unprotected to help the French, without receiving very much help in return. The time was now past when they would be satisfied with anything less than substantial improvements in Choctaw-French trade relations. Bienville was worried. Unable to live up to his promises that the Company would supply them with the things they needed, he warned the Regent: "It is to be feared that this nation of five to six thousand men which serves us as a rampart will let itself be corrupted by the English if the Company continues to leave this colony destitute of all assistance."[7]

Bienville had good reason to be alarmed. Scoff as they might about Law's botched attempts to colonize Louisiana, the English believed that the wave of new immigrants presented a menace to their own colonies, especially to Carolina. At a meeting of the Board of Trade in London, the former governor of South Carolina, Robert Johnson, warned that if a war should recur with France, Carolina would fall prey to them, and very probably Virginia, New York, and the other "Plantations" would feel the effects of the French growing so powerful in America. To wean the Choctaws from the French, the Carolinians were willing to haul trade goods right into the native villages, even at the risk of temporary financial loss. As their spokesman put it, a penny spent then might save pounds later and enable the English to dispossess the French in time of war. To forestall the encroachment of the English traders, the Louisiana Council agreed to give better terms to the Choctaws and to build a warehouse in their territory; and Antoine Huché, a long-time interpreter and ambassador to the nation, was sent along to keep abreast of developments and keep the nation in the French camp.

On another front, the Chickasaws were doing their best to "corrupt" the Choctaws. Pointing to the Yamasee War as an example, when attacks on the Carolinians had forced the English to adopt better trade practices, they urged the Choctaws to attack the French for the same reason. But no matter

[7]Bienville to the Regent, August 8, 1721, *MPA*, 3:307.

the blandishments, the Choctaws could not bring themselves to desert their old allies. Meanwhile, apparently at the instigation of English traders, some Chickasaw bands began to make sporadic attacks on French *voyageurs*. In 1721, and more frequently the following year, incidents of plunder and even murder occurred on the Mississippi. Two Frenchmen were killed in broad daylight on their way from the Illinois. In a raid on Fort St. Pierre at the Yazoos, a Sergeant Ritter and his wife were scalped and the fort plundered; and on his way back from a journey to the Arkansas, La Harpe barely managed to escape from another marauding war party. Fear of Chickasaw attacks even drove the Arkansas to abandon their old village, which had formerly been a stopping place for French convoys on their way up and down the river.

Although these raids were isolated events rather than outright warfare, they were particularly hard to counter: a quick musket shot from the river bank, a lightning dash from the shelter of woods or canebreaks and all could be over. Before the end of the year, Bienville also had disturbing news of clashes between the French and the Natchez near Fort Rosalie. Apart from the loss of life these assaults entailed, they disrupted trade on the river, which was bad for business, at a time when the Company was determined to wrest some return for the money it had poured into the colony.

Chapter VIII
The Company Tightens Its Hold

In December 1722, the provisional board of commissioners appointed by the Regent brought in their final blueprint for the Company of the Indies. Freed from royal supervision, the newly organized company was enabled to tighten its grip on Louisiana and put its own directors and its own policies in place. The Company's major goal was to get Louisiana's finances in order. To that end, it was imperative to bring some order into the confusion surrounding the colony's business and accounting procedures, ferret out waste and inefficiency, and force Company debtors to pay their bills. As well, Company employees found guilty of dishonesty would be severely dealt with. The commissioners also concerned themselves with the practice of religion. A contract was drawn up with the Capuchin Order of the Champagne province to exercise their ministry in Southern Louisiana, and the Jesuits retained their mission in the north. (Father Davion, the lone remaining priest of the Foreign Missions shortly returned to France.)

To implement the new reforms, the colonial administration was revamped yet again. For the time being, Bienville was retained as commandant general, but there would be no more directors or *ordonnateurs*[1]; Delorme, the sole remaining director, was removed from office. In place of directors, there would be two royal commissioners, Jacques de La Chaise and Jean-François Choplet de Sauvoy, who were to stay in the colony until they had straightened out the Company's tangled finances. Neither of these two men was empowered to sit on the Superior Council or the administrative council of the colony. For these bodies, six new councillors were appointed, each with his own responsibilities. Bienville, as commandant general and Leblond de La Tour as lieutenant general would serve respectively as chairman and vice chairman of both groups.

The new structure looked workable enough. Sauvoy and La Chaise would get all the outstanding accounts straightened out, get a proper bookkeeping system in place, rout out the cheats and profiteers, and return to France with their report. The senior councillor, Antoine Bruslé, would supervise public finances and the distribution of the presents which Bienville made to the Indians, as well as performing other duties relating to trade and wages. Jacques Fazende was appointed to oversee the warehouses and general shipping. The third-ranking councillor, Paul Perry, was named general inspector of stocks and bookkeeping and was also expected to encourage agriculture and mining. Sieur Masclary, who had already been

[1]The man who scrutinized the accounts and acted as paymaster.

serving as Company clerk in Biloxi, was appointed to conduct a general census and oversee records of births, marriages and deaths. The remaining councillor, Antoine Guilhet, was responsible for running the hospital and overseeing the missions.

Unfortunately, the scheme ran into difficulties before it got off the ground. Guilhet died before he could take office and his duties were given to Perry, who, ironically for an overseer of the missions, was suspected of being an atheist; and Bienville refused to allow Masclary to enter the council because he was allegedly a known brawler and general troublemaker. Perhaps the greatest loss to the colony was the death of Sauvoy, evidently a capable man, shortly after his arrival in New Orleans. Consequently, La Chaise was left to correct all the financial abuses on his own. La Chaise was a diligent man with a reputation for getting things done and following Company orders to the letter. That was his good side. The other side, even if we ignore his pettiness and lack of discretion, was his overbearing and malicious character. Not content with the troubles that came his way in the normal course of events, he went out of his way to create them. All in all, he was not the type of man likely to create harmony in the colony.

The *Galatée*, carrying the new commissioners, councillors, and lesser lights such as storekeepers and clerks, approached Ship Island on April 8, 1723. On the voyage out, La Chaise, who took his role of Grand Inquisitor very seriously, encountered his first setbacks. As he told it, Sieur Arnaud, a surgeon who "came on board with the pox" spent most of the voyage in bed, using up the Company's medicines and consuming two chickens a day. At Cap Français, Arnaud bestirred himself, went ashore, and bought five ancres of brandy, which he took on board contrary to Company rules. In spite of La Chaise's efforts—and they were considerable—Arnaud managed to hold on to the brandy. The commissioners were outwitted again at Biloxi. In order to catch the colonial leaders unawares, they intended to keep their own identity a secret until they reached the capital; so the boatman sent ashore for a pilot to guide the *Galatée* up the river was cautioned to hold his tongue. The post commandant, Henry de Louboey, was not to be fobbed off so easily. When his questions and his requests for provisions were turned aside, he boarded the ship himself with a large trunk, telling the unlikely story "that those were his clothes, and that it [the trunk] was always with him." In the end, through a series of complicated maneuvers, Louboey managed to find out the identity of the commissioners, and get a load of butter as well, which he doubtless sold on the black market. The great reform was getting off to a slow start!

The commissioners were foiled again in their efforts to steal a march on the authorities at New Orleans, in particular on Director Delorme who was suspected of fraud. Before disembarking at Biloxi to take the fastest route to

New Orleans, La Chaise and Sauvoy had all the incoming letters locked up on the *Galatée* to prevent news of the commissioners' identity from leaking out. Messengers from Bienville and Leblond de La Tour requesting official mail were even sent away empty-handed. All the precautions were in vain. On his arrival in New Orleans, La Chaise asked Bienville to have seals placed on Delorme's property, only to be told that it was a little late in the day for that. Somehow, Delorme had already been alerted. If any piastres had been illegally accumulated, as La Chaise suspected, they had been spirited away.

La Chaise's orderly soul was shocked when he saw the condition of the warehouse. The hurricane of the previous year had carried away the roof, leaving the merchandise exposed to the elements. Inside all was chaos. Guns were rusted; tools, nails and other odds and ends were scattered outside, all covered with water. After searching high and low, no register of expenditures or receipts was to be found. For this he held Delorme to blame, and by implication Bienville, who should have been more vigilant in his supervision. Bienville's explanation—that the directors did not want him meddling in what they considered their business—did not impress him.

Were it not for his overbearing ways, one could feel sorry for La Chaise. Getting anything done was a struggle. When he tried to get a roofer, he was told that there was no roofer in the colony. Good workers of any kind were scarce; and the few that were available were commandeered by the engineers who refused to give them up without a fight. Company merchandise was scattered in sites all over the colony, in Biloxi, in Leblond de La Tour's home, even in Father Davion's residence at the Balise. Half the time there were simply no invoices to verify the delivery of goods and no proper accounting system. All of this he blamed on the carelessness and skulduggery of the Louisiana officials, and undoubtedly there was plenty of that. But there were also extenuating circumstances—the chaos surrounding the Franco-Spanish war and the initial settlements at Old and New Biloxi; the hurricane of the previous year; the shortage of workers and materials, to name a few. There were also times when shipments from France came without invoices.

On top of everything, an epidemic which spread through the colony claimed many victims, including Sauvoy and Leblond de La Tour, both of whom would be dead in a few months. La Chaise himself and all the councillors were stricken and Delorme was at death's door. Around New Orleans alone there were more than 900 people ill at the same time, which delayed the inventory of the merchandise and did not improve La Chaise's disposition. However, by the end of October he was able to report that the inventory was complete "all in alphabetical order and very convenient."

To aid him in investigating employees suspected of milking the company, La Chaise resorted to a system of *monitories* occasionally used in France, but new to Louisiana. Based on the idea of individual conscience, *monitories* obliged anyone suspecting another of a crime to disclose the information to a priest. The priest then brought the matter to the attention of the civil authorities, whereupon the witness was secretly examined. Carried to its final conclusion, the accused was allowed to confront his accuser before a decision of guilt or innocence was rendered. With the cooperation of Father Raphael, the superior of the Capuchins, announcements of suspected crimes were made from the altar on three successive Sundays, and La Chaise waited to haul in his nets. Apparently the catch was less than expected. For this he held Bienville partially responsible. Bienville who had heard denunciations enough in his time and had been the subject of many more, had no stomach for *monitories*. Hearing that his servant Petit had denounced a storekeeper for watering the wine, he fired the accuser on the spot. Another man who stepped forward with accusations was the deputy registrar of the council, Jean-Baptiste Raguet. Apparently Raguet impeached the honor, the honesty, the loyalty, the justice of Messrs Bienville, Chateauguay, Hubert, Duvergier, Delorme, Le Gac, Larcebault, and Villardeau, in a word everyone who had conducted the affairs of the Company. Two years later when the process was coming to an end (and Bienville was back in France) Raguet apparently had a change of heart and claimed to have forgotten everything. Still, his original deposition was surely another nail in Bienville's coffin.

From the beginning, La Chaise went out of his way to excoriate the commandant; perhaps he felt free to do so because the Company had already voiced suspicions about him. Be that as it may, La Chaise's very first dispatch contained a litany of complaints and insinuations. While acknowledging that Bienville had lodged the two commissioners in his own house until they could find suitable accommodation, that he "had received nothing but courtesies from him" and in fact that he had "no reason to complain of him," he went on to assail him left and right. Prophet-like, he assured the directors that the Company would flourish if only Bienville and his relatives were removed. Without producing any evidence at all, he asserted that Bienville was generally hated. In the next breath he claimed that the commandant had far too much influence over the councillors and that "no matter what resolutions they have made together he [Bienville] only had to say one word, and he made them all change." He even accused him of wishing to bring about the downfall of the colony "in order that the king might take control of it and that Bienville might be able to do what he wished."[2] Never a man to appraise a situation before making pronouncements, he poured out a long screed of complaints, many of them based on hearsay or on the word of known malcontents. Phrases such as "I am not sure that this is true" or "I have heard many times" or "on the report of those that were there" do nothing to mitigate the cumulative effect of the charges. A pattern was set up in his correspondence: those who complained about Bienville, particularly "people of quality" were unfortunate victims of the commandant's malevolence, and those who sided with him were dupes or rascals.

A case in point was the young scapegrace Jean-Baptiste de Chavannes who, according to La Chaise, came from "honorable and rich people" but who had "the misfortune of killing one of his friends in a duel" over a woman. Bienville refused the position of secretary to the council to Sieur de Chavannes for frivolous reasons, according to La Chaise. (The same Chavannes was later fired by Commandant Périer because he was "indiscreet and of a very bad spirit" besides knowing nothing about his job). Another of La Chaise's protégés was the young officer Dumont de Montigny, a one-time smuggler and ne'er-do-well with a gift for words. (He wrote a history of Louisiana after his return to France.) Bienville considered him "a bad fellow and slovenly" and refused to give him a commission as an officer, no matter how much La Chaise complained. Evidently Bienville's judgment was only too correct, for Commandant Périer was later authorized to cashier Montigny as being unworthy of the service. La Chaise's French heart was revolted by Bienville's favoritism for the Canadians over the French. Carried away with sympathy for his ill-treated countrymen, he went on to complain that "he [Bienville] has spoiled the Indians by taking their side against the French." As for Bienville's vaunted influence over the same Indians, La Chaise assured the Company that there were others in the colony who could manage them as well, if not better.

He even went so far as to blame Bienville's "slackness," if not out and out complicity, for a rebellion among the troops. What happened was this: La Chaise had orders from the Company to cut down on the soldiers' pay and rations, pathetic enough as they were, as even he himself admitted. Bienville knew only too well from the revolts of the previous year that the ill-clad, ill-housed, and ill-fed soldiers would revolt if the ordinance was carried into effect. In spite of his remonstrances, for which he had the backing of the council, La Chaise insisted on following the letter of the law. The inevitable happened: the troops marched in a body to Bruslé's residence and threatened him with force. To forestall a full-scale rebellion,

[2]See e.g., La Chaise to the Directors, *MPA*, 2:294-391.

the order had to be rescinded. Still, La Chaise laid the blame at Bienville's door for not cutting the rations earlier on.

Many of the officers owed huge sums to the Company, but to get them to pay was another matter. Those with the largest debts, such as Captains D'Arensbourg and De Blanc were suspended and Major Pailloux was recalled, but whether the Company ever recovered any of the debts is doubtful. In his anxiety to turn a profit for the Company, La Chaise also boosted prices for Company merchandise, so that many debtors discovered that they owed more than expected. To make matters worse, the piastre, which was in common currency in the colony, was heavily discounted in the Company stores.

The French directors were delighted with their new broom. The more complaints they heard about disorders and peculation, the more they felt that they had finally found someone who could be trusted to keep his eyes open and his hands out of the till. Better accounting practices were being put into effect and those employees found to be incompetent or dishonest were being replaced by worthy men. Or so it seemed. Alas, La Chaise was a notoriously bad judge of character. Several of his choices turned out to be worse than their predecessors. François Duval, whom he promoted to the post of auditor of accounts and later chief cashier, against the wishes of the council "because they let themselves be won over by Mr. de Bienville" later ended up owing the Company 120,000 *livres,* most of which was never recovered.

Bienville's own judgment was to be shortly questioned in his handling of an outbreak of hostilities in the Natchez territory. This beautiful rolling country had attracted the attention of several settlers. By 1722 there were more than 100 French people and several slaves living and working on the two major concessions in the area, St. Catherine, originally owned by Hubert and now in the hands of a syndicate; and a Company concession called The White Earth. Smaller concessions, including the holding of Le Page du Pratz, were also springing up in the area close to Fort Rosalie. By all accounts, the Natchez welcomed the arrival of the French and helped supply them with food while they were awaiting their first harvest. On their side, the natives were glad to trade with the French for gunpowder, brandy, cloth, and other merchandise. But relations, so good on the surface, shortly began to show signs of strain. Accounts differ somewhat as to what triggered the conflict. Apparently the second in command at Saint Catherine's, Captain Guenot, offended the natives by putting an honored man in chains for some offense or other. Whatever the reason, or combination of reasons, a house on the concession was attacked in the summer of 1722 and other skirmishes followed throughout the summer and fall. Matters came to a head in October when a certain Sergeant Fontaine took an old warrior to task about a debt. An argument ensued and the old man was shot and killed. Common justice and prudence demanded that Sergeant Fontaine should have been punished severely, instead of which he received a mere slap on the wrist from Commandant Berneval.

Unfortunately, the murdered man belonged to the Apple Village, where the residents had no great love for the French. Ancient Hair, the chief of the village ordered his braves to attack the St. Catherine concession. The first victim was Guenot, who was ambushed on his way from Fort Rosalie to St. Catherine. Other ambushes followed; cattle, horses and pigs were slaughtered and no one dared to go out to work in the fields. With his little contingent of 20 soldiers and 200 nervous settlers, there was little the post commandant could do against several hundred warriors, so he dispatched Captain Du Tisné to New Orleans for help.

Meanwhile Stung Serpent, the old reliable friend of the French, set to work to settle the dispute. In a few days, hostilities ceased, the peace calumet was passed around, and life returned, more or less, to normal.

Fearful of a French counterstrike, Stung Serpent accompanied by several other chiefs, set out for New Orleans to talk to Bienville. Bienville, who was very ill at the time, left instructions for Leblond de La Tour that the chiefs were to be treated with all courtesy. On Bienville's behalf, they were to be given the customary presents, and more, on the understanding that they would bring an end to the fighting. La Tour, who was all for arresting the delegation and dispatching an army to cow the Natchez, reluctantly bowed to his superior's decision. Undoubtedly, the last thing Bienville wanted was a large scale offensive against the Natchez with the Choctaw-Chickasaw war still simmering. Moreover, with his rag-tag army of soldiers unaccustomed to frontier fighting, the campaign might well turn into a rout. He also knew, as he later explained, that the Indians did not let themselves be besieged in their villages and that it would be absolutely impossible to pursue them in the woods and the canes without the assistance of some Indian allies.

Among those allies, he surely counted Stung Serpent and his followers. The chiefs returned home on the understanding that they would bring the offending Natchez to heel, and Major Pailloux was dispatched to the village with a force of sixty recruits to reinforce the garrison.

When Pailloux and his men arrived at the Natchez in late November, the troubles appeared to be over. At this point, the story becomes somewhat murky. Apparently, the settlers expected firmer measures to be taken against the guilty Natchez. Certainly some retribution was in order if only to save face. But Pailloux asked for little in the way of compensation, perhaps leaving it to the good offices of Stung Serpent. Be that as it may, after about a week he judged it safe to return to New Orleans.

Shortly thereafter the disturbances began to flare up again at the St. Catherine concession. The natives stopped short of murder or personal attacks on the inhabitants, concentrating their efforts on looting, and killing livestock. Still it was an untenable situation. Crops were lost because the black slaves could not go out to the fields, and the people lived in a constant state of terror, because the scattered homesteads were very vulnerable to attack, and the rotting old Fort Rosalie could afford little protection in the event of a major onslaught.

In the spring of 1723, the settlers again appealed for help. The response of the Superior Council fell far short of what they expected: there was to be no more trading with the Natchez and no weapons of any kind were to be sold to them. The following month a competent officer named Charles Desliettes was sent off to the area with a small force of twenty-three men. Still the violence continued and escalated. The emboldened attackers even began to jeer at the French to their face, and armed warriors staged a mock peace ceremony before the demoralized settlers.

It was time for Bienville himself to intervene, past time as far as Leblond de La Tour was concerned, who chastised him bitterly for not having taken action sooner. (On the other hand, Le Page du Pratz, who lived through the whole fracas, criticized Bienville for coming at all.) One cannot be sure why Bienville let the matter drag out so long. In the beginning he relied on the good offices of Stung Serpent, but when those failed, why did he wait almost a year before taking his usual decisive action? The sorry military situation undoubtedly played a part. He himself also put down the delay to the time of the planting of the crops, so precious to the French and to the Indians, to the overflow of the river and the shortage of boats. He may also have decided to wait it out until the time of the annual Corn Festival in October when most of the Natchez would be in the Great Village and more vulnerable to sudden assault.

Finally, in August 1723, Bienville came to the council with a proposal to exact vengeance on the Natchez. All the councillors agreed that the arrogance of the Natchez could no longer be tolerated without bringing the whole colony into disrepute, all except Leblond de La Tour who refused to vote one way or another. In his opinion, Bienville brought the matter before the council only to shift the blame for a campaign which was far too late to be successful.

In any event, Bienville gathered together a small army of soldiers and native allies and set out for the Natchez territory in late September. On his arrival at the post, he found Stung Serpent and the other native leaders waiting to speak to him, having refused to deal with Desliettes or with anyone else. With their active assistance, the Apple Village was attacked and subdued. In a few days the fighting was over. Bienville insisted that

Ancient Hair, and the other ringleaders be executed, and that the executions be carried out by the Indians themselves. The Natchez also agreed to incorporate the Apple Village into the other villages, and they undertook to live in harmony with the French. If they had a grievance against an inhabitant they promised not to take matters into their own hands, but to take it to the commandant for settlement. Lastly, they undertook to indemnify St. Catherine's for the losses the concession had sustained.

With this agreement ratified, life at the Natchez returned to normal and the French were able to go about their business in peace. Yet there were ominous signs of possible trouble ahead. In his report to the council, Bienville did not hesitate to blame the French for most of the troubles. Even the Indians of the Apple Village were partially exonerated because of the beatings and bad treatment they had sustained at the hands of greedy Frenchmen. Later, when he was back in France, he warned the Company that there could be more trouble if the French settlers continued to mix too freely with the Natchez, and he recommended that the battered old fort should be torn down and a new one erected. But with the Company intent on making money, Indian affairs were relegated to second place and the natives were exploited and taken for granted, which was to cost the Company and Louisiana dearly in the long run.

While Bienville was settling the Natchez affair, the Company was planning his recall. The directive came in the guise of a leave of absence. Ostensibly, he was being summoned to France for consultation about colonial affairs; in reality, he was being recalled for good, and he knew it. As far as the businessmen at Company headquarters were concerned, Bienville had outlived his usefulness. Slowly but surely, they were edging their way to rid the colony of those who might tend to interfere with Company business and Bienville was first on the list. His long years of service were more of a liability than an asset, for they might encourage him to think that he knew how to run the colony better than the Company officials. The Company wanted its own men in key positions, men like La Chaise, whom they could trust to follow directions, and Bienville was far too independent for that. His expertise with the Indians even worked against him. The few skirmishes here and there were nothing like the bloody conflicts on the Canadian border, or the Yamasee massacres in South Carolina. As the Company saw it, the Louisiana Indians obviously liked the French, so a new leader should have no difficulty with them.

Whether the complaints of former directors had any hand in his recall is a moot point. Certainly Hubert and his wife wrote scathing denunciations of Bienville on their return to France, but Hubert was an embittered man who had lost all his effects in a shipwreck. La Chaise's denunciations would also have arrived too late to influence the company's decision, though no doubt they confirmed the directors in the view that Bienville should never see Louisiana again.

Until a permanent appointment was made, the man chosen to replace Bienville was Pierre Dugué de Boisbriant, commandant in the Illinois area. Since it could take months for despatches from New Orleans to reach Boisbriant and allow him to come downriver, Leblond de La Tour was ordered to hold the fort until his arrival. By the time word of the change reached Louisiana, Leblond de La Tour was dead, and Bienville carried on until he had his next orders. Later that year the orders came: Chateauguay was to take over and Bienville was to return on the *Bellone*. However, Chateauguay was so ill at the time that he was in no condition to take over, so Bienville postponed his departure until Boisbriant arrived in January. One of his last acts was to bring about a treaty between the Chickasaws, the Choctaws, and the French.

La Chaise could hardly wait for Bienville's departure. Ungracious to the last, he kept importuning him to say exactly when he would leave. Bienville made his feelings clear about this insulting behavior in a stinging letter to the commissioner. Then, on January 23, 1725, he signed the council book for the last time, and in March he and his brother boarded the *Bellone* for France, a country he had visited only once in his life, at the age of eighteen.

The *Bellone*, laden with a valuable cargo of indigo, pitch, and piastres sailed down the Mississippi into the Gulf of Mexico. Just off Dauphin Island it hit a sandbar and sank, taking all the goods, including Bienville's papers, to the bottom of the sea. Fortunately a nearby brigantine rescued all but two of the passengers. Two months passed by before the rescued passengers sailed off to France on the *Gironde*.

Early in August Bienville and his brother stepped off the boat at L'Orient. The Atlantic crossing was particularly hard on Chateauguay, weak as he was from his earlier illness, and Bienville waited for him to recover before proceeding to Paris. In the meantime, he wrote to the navy minister advising him that he would soon report to Paris and hinting at a possible reward for almost twenty-seven years of service in Louisiana.

Chapter IX
Bienville in France

Major changes had taken place in France by the time Bienville arrived on the scene. The Prince Regent was dead and the series of councils he had set up had been abolished, so that half a dozen ministers again administered the country. Replacing the Navy Council was Jean Frédéric Phélypeaux, Comte de Maurepas. Knowing full well that he was out of favor with the Company of the Indies, Bienville may have allowed himself to hope that Maurepas would intervene on his behalf or, if the worst came to the worst, find him a posting in another French colony.

It soon became clear that most of the Company directors were adamantly opposed to any suggestion of reinstating him. He had to be pushed aside in order to make way for a man of their own choosing, who could work in harmony with La Chaise and end the divisions in the colony. Nonetheless, the controller-general, Charles-Gaspard Dodun was quick to give credit where credit was due: "I must give justice to M. de Bienville," he wrote to the minister. "He is a man of courage and a good officer; and although as a matter of fact it would not be good to let him go on as commandant, there is in this position no attack on his honor or honesty, and he could indeed be capable of serving well in all other posts to which you could name him."[1]

While the directors were looking around for a new commandant more to their liking, they consulted Bienville about the situation in Louisiana. Perhaps his reply told them more than they wanted to hear. In a long memorandum which he presented to Maurepas and to the Company, he dealt with everything from agriculture, to trade, to conditions at the posts, to the administration of justice.

As a military man, he saw the colony's conciliar system of government as a kind of democracy gone mad. Poor inhabitants with a problem or a grievance had to leave their farms and waste time and money, and perhaps risk their lives, to go to New Orleans and wait for the council to assemble, and when the councillors did get together it took them an eternity to make up their minds about the most trivial matters. Urgent needs at remote posts could not be satisfied on time. As he wrote:

> I agree that several opinions reconciled with each other may produce a decision more correct than a single one, but also how many projects are there which come to grief . . . when they are not conducted and

[1]Cited in Charles O'Neill, *Church and State in French Colonial Louisiana: Policy and Politics to 1732* (New Haven, 1966), 180.

> concluded with celerity which alone often constitutes their success and always diminishes their expense?[2]

In his opinion, the councillors knew little or nothing about the specific tasks assigned to them and paid too much attention to their own private affairs until, as he put it, "I have been so disgusted with their slowness and their indifference that I have remained in a sort of state of inactivity." To his mind the council should be abolished entirely and replaced by a commandant and an intendant. He also urged the Company to pay a decent wage to all their employees so that they would not have to resort to "certain expedients" to make ends meet.

The directors could hardly have been pleased at Bienville's blunt opinion that the Company's own lack of foresight in sending out "such a prodigious number of people all at the same time" was largely responsible for the misery of the early immigrants. And, he argued, many of them were the wrong kind of people. "Instead of filling the concessions with so many managers, controllers, warehouse keepers, bookkeepers, and foremen," he told them, they should have sent out more workmen and slaves. In his opinion, the cost of feeding and transporting the many convicts and idlers had also put an impossible strain on the colony's scarce resources.

Despite everything, he was optimistic about the future of Louisiana. The fertile land could grow rice, corn, tobacco and a host of other crops; and the Illinois mines could be profitably exploited when the country had enough workers and enough food to feed them. So long as the Company was content with a modest profit at first, or even sacrificed profit altogether for a year or two, the rewards would be great.

Whatever the directors may have felt about some parts of the memoir, they must have valued the section dealing with the native people. In meticulous detail, he described every nation and tribe—their situation, their way of life, their medicines, and their attitude towards the French. He was emphatic about the need for more missionaries among the Indians, even if his interest lay more in the temporal than in the spiritual role of the priests:

> I cannot too earnestly recommend to the Company that it is necessary to have some missionaries among the big Indian nations, for in addition to the knowledge of God that they would impart to them, at least to some of them, nothing is more useful than a missionary to retain the Indians, to learn what is happening among them, and to inform the commandants of the neighbouring posts about it, to prevent the quarrels that may arise between the voyageurs and the

[2] Memoir on Louisiana [by Bienville] 1725, *MPA*, 3:501-2.

> Indians, and especially to see to it that the former do not sell their goods at too high a price.[3]

Bienville also presented Maurepas with an account of his long service to the Crown, no doubt hoping that the minister would use his influence on his behalf. Known later to be a competent man, even if "he wouldn't know the sea if he saw it" as one wag put it, the twenty-five-year-old navy minister was the son of former minister Pontchartrain. Maurepas cannot fail to have been impressed with Bienville's twenty-seven-year record of trials and triumphs, but he was never known to go out on a limb for anyone, least of all for a controversial figure like Bienville. Perhaps his father's suspicions of the ex-commandant also carried some weight.

In August 1726, Étienne Périer, a naval ensign employed by the Company of the Indies, was appointed commandant of Louisiana. Bienville's disgrace was complete. At the age of forty-six, he was relegated to the sidelines in a country he hardly knew, knowing that he could never hope for a leadership position in Louisiana as long as the colony was in Company hands. Comptroller Dodun again spoke up in his favor and it was Dodun who persuaded the prime minister, the duc de Bourbon, to grant him a pension of 3,000 *livres* a year. With that, and the quite modest sum of 60,000 *livres* which he had accumulated over the years, he was able to live comfortably enough.

Bienville's relatives and supporters in Louisiana also felt the sting of Company disapproval. His brother Chateauguay was stripped of his position as king's lieutenant, his two De Noyan nephews were cashiered, and his cousin Boisbriant was ordered back to France. One by one, all "Bienvillists" were either disgraced or fell into line.

Very little is known about how Bienville passed his days in Paris. In the 1720s Paris was a bustling city with a population of about 800,000 people lured there by business opportunities and pleasure of every sort—operas, theaters, balls, and all the glitter of fashionable life. For a person with money and a taste for high life, Paris was the place to be, but it was hardly a place where Bienville could feel at home. Accustomed to command, he was now a colonial has-been, a mere nobody as far as Parisian society was concerned. He kept up his relationship with his old friends, the Jesuits, to whom he sold a parcel of his land near New Orleans. For two years he also enjoyed the companionship of his brother Chateauguay. When the latter obtained an appointment as king's lieutenant in Martinique, he accompanied him as far as Rochefort, where Sérigny was governor. The

[3] Memoir on Louisiana, *MPA*, 3:515.

three men and their older brother Baron de Longueuil, then governor of Montreal, were the sole survivors of the ten Le Moyne brothers.

Whether Bienville ever heard of it or not, there were calls, from what might be seen as an unlikely source, for his appointment to succeed his brother Longueuil as governor of Montreal, when the latter died in 1729. Over the years, the Iroquois had come to trust and respect the Le Moynes so much that they had "adopted" Longueuil and his brother Maricourt as their sons, so when Longueuil died they petitioned Governor Charles de la Boische de Beauharnois of Canada to have Bienville succeed him. It is hardly necessary to say that the request went unheeded.

Meanwhile, during his enforced retirement, Bienville kept abreast of developments in Louisiana. His nephew, Gilles-Augustin Payen de Noyan managed his concessions, and sold or leased property on his uncle's orders. Through other sources, including his good friend, Jesuit priest Father Nicolas Beaubois, he learned that to be labelled as pro-Bienville was the kiss of death for anyone wishing to make a name for himself in the colony. That he deeply resented the malevolence of Company officials goes without saying. He had six years to nurse his grievances before the king called him out of retirement because of a calamity that had befallen Louisiana.

Chapter X
Périer at the Helm

The man who replaced Bienville was Étienne de Périer, a naval ensign who had fought gallantly in the War of the Spanish Succession and later entered the service of the Company of the Indies. Universally praised for his bravery and good judgment, he seemed to be the ideal person to bring the rebellious elements in the military into line and clean up the disorders in the colony. As a Company employee, he could also be expected to carry out Company policy and get along with La Chaise, whom the directors saw as the beleaguered victim of disgruntled Bienvillists. To make his task easier, the Company purged the Louisiana Council of undesirable elements. Rebellious councillors Perault, Perry, and Fazende were dismissed for taking sides against La Chaise, whom they accused of trickery and authoritarianism. The ousted men were replaced by Company clerks, Louis Bru, Raymond Dauseville, and Marc-Antoine de Loire des Ursins; and Diron Dartaguiette (brother of Company syndic and former commissary of Louisiana, Martin Dartaguiette) replaced Chateauguay as king's lieutenant and commandant of Fort Condé.

From the outset, Périer showed that he meant business. He cracked down on unruly military officers who had overstepped their authority and he brought other dissidents in line. Post commanders were ordered to send known criminals to New Orleans, where they were severely punished, and in extreme cases put to death. Women who persisted in leading scandalous lives were flogged by the soldiers—rather ironical, considering that many of the same soldiers very likely contributed to the girls' bad behavior in the first place. Brawling, public drunkenness, and theft were also harshly dealt with. In a few months, peace and good order prevailed in the colony. Even the Jesuit priest, Father Nicolas Beaubois, a particular friend of Bienville, was delighted with the change; and Father Raphael, the Capuchin superior could hardly restrain his praise for the new commandant. "He has done more for the State and religion than we had previously dared to hope for," he wrote. By his own account, Périer played no favorites; he listened to both sides in a dispute, but never became embroiled himself. He also assured the directors that he was determined to work in harmony with La Chaise.

The new commandant foresaw a bright future for Louisiana. Of course there were the usual drawbacks—there were never enough slaves, or enough skilled workmen, or enough funds to complete all the projects that had to be done. And try as he would, he could not prevent misunderstandings from arising between Father Beaubois and Father Raphael, who was afraid of Jesuit encroachment on the Capuchin missions. Very soon, cracks also developed in Périer's hitherto "perfect understanding" with La Chaise. A little malicious gossip here, a little double dealing there, and La Chaise's out-and-out hostility toward the Jesuits and the Ursuline nuns who had recently arrived in New Orleans—all of these offended Périer until he finally lost all respect for the commissioner. Still, for the good of the colony, he tried to keep his feelings to himself.

On the whole, the commandant was happy with the way things were going. More and more people were raising tobacco, especially in the Natchez area, and the colony was almost self-sufficient in agricultural products. For this he allotted a great deal of credit to himself. With a tacit allusion to Bienville and Iberville, he criticized "earlier leaders" for placing the main settlement at Mobile rather than on the Mississippi. Had matters been in his hands, he assured the Company, he would have managed to get the ships up the Mississippi, and all the confusion and loss of life at Biloxi would have been avoided.

Like many people before and since, Périer fancied himself in the one area where he was at his worst, the management of Indian affairs. Having a goodly share of natural vanity, he was convinced of his talent for handling the Indians, even though he had never met an Indian in his life before he arrived in Louisiana. The fine welcoming speeches made to him by a few friendly chiefs on his arrival in the colony led him to the simplistic conclusion that all the natives were equally well disposed towards the French and particularly towards himself. Soon he was boasting that he was more capable of managing the tribes than Bienville ever was.

The same belief brought him into conflict with Diron Dartaguiette. Dartaguiette, who had exclusive trading rights with the Choctaws, was in the habit of hiring traders to travel to the villages, exchanging furs for trade goods. As we know, French trade goods were never as good or as cheap as the English variety, so a number of Choctaws began to do business with the Carolinians. Rightly or wrongly, Périer became convinced that Dartaguiette was throwing the natives into the arms of the Carolinians by treating them badly and overcharging them for trade goods. In August 1729, he sent an officer named Régis Roullet among the tribe to find out the cause of their grievances and to rid the villages of English traders. Périer could not have made a more unfortunate choice. Roullet was haughty and ham-fisted, "neither loved nor respected by the Choctaws." Not surprisingly, the mission was handled with all the finesse of a bull in a china shop. Presenting himself as the Indians' friend and protector, Roullet invited the chiefs to bring him their grievances against Dartaguiette, which naturally they were not slow to do if it would mean a better deal for themselves. But by depicting Dartaguiette as an exploiter, even to the extent of predicting his recall to France, he did more harm than good. The open revelation of divisions in the French leadership was unlikely to inspire the respect of the Indians. Roullet further violated the native sense of decorum by beating Dartaguiette's interpreter, whom he accused of coming to a meeting to spy on the proceedings. (It was characteristic of the Indians that they never beat their young men.) In New Orleans, Périer compounded the problem by his over-eagerness to comply with the demands of the Choctaw delegates sent on by Roullet, even going to the extent of promising to bring down the price of trade goods to the English level, something the Company could not hope to deliver. The Choctaws, who were well attuned to the nuances of French behavior, correctly sensed the colony's dependence on their good graces, so they continued to escalate their demands, and when the demands went unmet they began to treat the French with contempt. In the short run, Périer's generosity brought most of the Choctaws into the French camp, even as it laid the groundwork for future discontent. And it is possible that the bitter division between Périer and the very touchy Dartaguiette adversely affected the unhappy events that were soon to follow.

On November 28, 1729, Louisiana was plunged into an all out war for the first time in its history. Before hostilities came to an end, much blood was spilt on both sides and the whole system of French-native alliances was disrupted. In the process, the Natchez nation was also wiped out and many of the pitiful survivors sold into slavery.

The immediate cause of the war was the high-handed behavior of the French commandant at Fort Rosalie, Captain Detchéparre. This same Detchéparre had taken time to settle a private quarrel with a duel, in which both men were wounded, at the height of the second Natchez "war," when the post needed all the defenders it could muster. Apparently Detchéparre had subsequently been called on the carpet several times for his drinking and debauchery and for his tyrannical behavior toward the native people. For some reason, however, he had found favor with Périer, who gave him the appointment over the head of engineer Ignace Broutin, whom the king had designated for the post in 1727. On the face of it, Périer's decision seems incomprehensible. There had been trouble at the Natchez post twice before, and Bienville had pegged it as a potential powder keg in his memoir to the Company directors, which Périer had read before his arrival in the colony. It will also be remembered that Bienville had held the French partly responsible for the disturbances of 1722-23. What the post obviously needed was a firm and tactful commandant who knew how to make himself respected by the Natchez and the French.

In the past, Bienville had been fortunate enough to have the Great Sun and his brother, Stung Serpent, to help mediate disputes, but the two men died in 1725. The Great Sun who succeeded them was a young man whom the French leaders hardly knew, or bothered to know. Périer himself had never visited the Natchez post, or indeed any of the posts, although the Company had urged him to do so. In the absence of any overt hostilities in the area, the authorities in New Orleans apparently assumed that there was nothing to worry about. Yet there were signs of trouble ahead. According to Le Page du Pratz, even Stung Serpent had become disillusioned with the French shortly before his death:

> What need did we have of the French? Do you think that before them we were not living better than we do now that we deprive ourselves of a part of our corn, game and fish which we kill for them even when we need them? Was it their guns? We used to use our bows and arrows which sufficed in providing us a good living. Was it their clothing, white, blue and red? We have animal skins which are warmer. . . . Before the arrival of the French we were living as men who knew how to survive with what we have, in place of this, today we are walking as slaves.[1]

If even Stung Serpent was becoming so disillusioned, the Franco-Natchez alliance was far from secure. As more French settlers arrived in the area, the Natchez began to feel squeezed out. The newcomers also began to mix far too freely with the natives, which made the Natchez uneasy because they were fond of solitude. In time, tensions built up about debts owed by the Indians for goods bought on credit, or about the cheating and insensitivity of some of the French, the commandant himself being the worst offender. As it stood, the situation was a disaster waiting to happen unless the French kept more to their own sector, as Bienville had recommended to the Company. Had there been a Jesuit priest in the area, he would have learned the native language and perhaps acted as a restraining influence on both sides. Unfortunately, the Capuchin priest Father Philibert ministered only to the settlers, and he had little or no influence even over them. The Great Sun who lacked the prestige of his father also felt powerless to intervene.

The seething discontent boiled over at the Great Corn Feast in November 1729. Detchéparre had demanded land from the chief of the Apple Village, threatening to destroy the village if his demands were not met. This display of contempt for Natchez rights could not be tolerated, especially by the chief of a village which had crossed swords with the French in the past. Speaking to an assembly of elders, the chief urged them to band together and rid their lands of every last French man, woman, and

[1]Le Page du Pratz, *History of Louisiana*. Translated from the French of M. Le Page du Pratz with some notes and observations (London, 1774), 21.

child. The next step was to win over the Great Sun to the scheme. Of what use was it for the Sun to appeal to the authorities in New Orleans against the tyranny of Detchéparre, he asked the chief. According to Le Page du Pratz, the young man was told

> [that] as long as the Great Sun, his father, and his uncle, the Stung Serpent, lived, the Commandant of the fort durst never undertake anything to their detriment; because the grand Chief of the French (Bienville) who resided at their great village (New Orleans) had a love for them; but that he the Great Sun, being unknown to the French, and but a youth, would be despised.[2]

The Great Sun was won over.

In the course of the next few days, Detchéparre apparently received repeated warnings of a possible Natchez uprising, from settlers, from a native man who had hunted for Bienville in the past, even from a Natchez princess. Evidently the commandant's stupidity exceeded even his brutality, for he did nothing to put his men on guard and made no attempt to placate the Natchez. It is even said that he spent the night before the massacre drinking and carousing in the Natchez village until dawn.

The following morning the axe fell. Bands of Natchez laden with game appeared at the fort and in the neighboring houses, on the pretext that they were returning from the hunt. As was quite common, they also asked to borrow some guns which the unsuspecting settlers gave them. At a given signal, they turned the guns on the French. The hated Detchéparre was among the first to be killed. By sunset, about 200 settlers lay dead and most of the women and children and 150 black slaves were held hostage. A young Jesuit priest, Father Poisson, who happened to be passing through on his way to his Arkansas mission was also killed while he stopped to attend to the wounded. (Interestingly, there is no mention of any such service by Father Philibert, who succeeded in escaping to New Orleans.) After the massacre the plunder began. Houses were levelled and a recently arrived ship laden with food and merchandise was captured. From the Natchez village the revolt was carried to the Yazoo where the French met the same fate.

A few Frenchmen who escaped the carnage carried the tale of horror to New Orleans. Panic spread throughout the colony. The Chickasaws, perhaps egged on by the English, were known to have helped foment the conspiracy; even the Choctaws were not free from suspicion.

[2]Le Page du Pratz, *History of Louisiana,* 78.

A general conspiracy could spell the end of the colony. New Orleans had no defenses at all and the scattered settlements were wide open to attack. In the paranoia of the moment every Indian was a potential enemy. Apparently without a qualm, Périer had black slaves massacre the Chouaches, a small neighboring tribe, in the hope of intimidating other little nations who might be thinking of banding against the French. He would even have meted out the same fate to other small nations who were "of no use" to the French had he not been afraid that the blacks might turn against their masters. It was a long way from Iberville's *Pax Gallica*.

Meanwhile he dispatched Captain François-Louis de Merveilleux up river to warn the settlers to be on their guard and to entrench themselves as best they could, and he followed this up by sending a few reliable men to organize groups of militia in the larger settlements. A ditch was hastily dug around New Orleans and military companies organized to defend the town. Reckoning that he had only about sixty men capable of taking the field against the Natchez, he hastily petitioned France to send out some troops under the command of his brother, Périer de Salvert.

Feeling that his presence was needed in New Orleans, Périer chose not to lead the army personally. To be sure he was later criticized for this. It cannot be denied that the Indian allies expected the great chief of the French to lead his men into battle; he might also have inspired the men with more fervor and made the Choctaws more tractable. Be that as it may, he eventually chose Henry de Louboey to lead the punitive expedition, after first accepting and then rejecting the services of Diron Dartaguiette. As king's lieutenant and a man who claimed to be able to rally the Choctaws behind him, Dartaguiette was furious at being relegated to Mobile. In his mind, it was all too clear that Périer had not put aside his animosity about the skin trade.

With all due respect to Louboey, who was an experienced post commandant, Périer was sending a boy on a man's errand. What the occasion called for was a strict disciplinarian who could keep a rag-tag conglomeration of soldiers, settlers, and Indians in order and keep them on the move. Instead, Louboey was slow to make decisions and too lenient to maintain order in the ranks. Throughout the campaign soldiers engaged in petty trading with the local Indians, a practice they kept up even with the Natchez. And when his troops were moving forward under cover of darkness, rather than proceeding cautiously as the situation demanded, they made enough noise to alert the enemy.

On their arrival at the Tunica village where they were supposed to rendezvous with the Choctaws, they dug trenches and waited, and waited, but no Choctaws appeared. In reality, the Choctaws were long gone. A force of about 550 led by Bienville's cousin, Charles Le Sueur, had proceeded up the well-known Natchez trail to the Natchez villages. Catching the warriors off guard outside their forts, Le Sueur and the Choctaws went on the attack at dawn on January 27. Before the Natchez were able to retreat into their forts, 80 of their warriors were killed and 60 French women and children and about 100 black prisoners were rescued. Some of the blacks, fearful of the fate that might await them at the hands of the Choctaws, elected to stay with the Natchez and fought side-by-side with them.

Runners were immediately dispatched to Louboey at the Tunica encampment. On his arrival at the scene on February 8, plans were made for a major onslaught. From the French point of view the siege was a disaster. The trenches were placed too low and the range was too great for the big guns, so that not a single stake in the Natchez fortifications was knocked down. Suddenly on the morning of February 22, 300 Natchez burst out of the fort in three different places and attacked the French in the trenches. Several soldiers threw down their arms and fled, but the bravery of a settler named Jean-François Delay and a group of other settlers managed to avert what could have been a massacre. Captain Pierre Dartaguiette, the youngest of the three Dartaguiette brothers, also fought with great distinction. As the siege dragged on, the Choctaws became disgusted with the poor showing of the French, and Louboey's men became more and more undisciplined. Finally a Choctaw chief named Alabama Mingo began to hurl insults at the Natchez, ordering them to give up the remaining prisoners before the guns were moved closer and their forts destroyed. The Natchez responded by offering to return the prisoners, on condition that the guns were moved back and the siege raised while negotiations were in progress, a demand to which Louboey agreed. But the Natchez had another trick up their sleeves. While the negotiations continued, the main force escaped from the fort and slipped away to the western bank of the river.

After the siege, the Choctaws returned to their villages carrying their dead and wounded warriors, and bringing with them the slaves that had been recaptured from the Natchez. For the natives, the expedition had been a disillusionment. To say the least, the French soldiers had not distinguished themselves in the siege, and the great French guns made terrible sounds but no impact. The Choctaws had borne the brunt of the fighting without being able to capture any booty from the Natchez and with little in the way of compensation from the French. Essentially they were mercenaries for the white men and they naturally expected to be paid for their efforts, so they felt quite justified in holding the black slaves as bargaining chips until they could wring good terms from their former allies. It took much cajolement and promises of future rewards before the Choctaws were mollified; even then neither side fully trusted the other again. The Choctaws felt that they had been exploited, and Périer was disgusted with what he considered to be their insolence.

Meanwhile Périer's brother had arrived in the colony with 150 men and preparations were made to rout out the remaining Natchez, but finding them was to prove no easy task. After a long and painful journey through swamps and marshes in bitter January weather, the camp was discovered on the Black River in present-day Concordia Parish of Louisiana. Luckily, the French managed to surround the camp before their presence was detected. Three days after the siege commenced, the Natchez surrendered and agreed to return their prisoners, on the understanding that their own lives would be spared. After the prisoners were returned, the Natchez filed out of the fort—450 women and fifty men, the discrepancy due to the fact that a large number of warriors had escaped during the night. The French had been duped again. The Périer brothers believed, or pretended to believe, that the nation was almost completely destroyed, and the weary army returned to New Orleans, whence Périer de Salvert shortly departed for France.

It soon became obvious that the Natchez had a good-sized fighting force left. Périer de Salvert's ship had hardly left the harbor before they were on the warpath again. Over 200 Natchez hunters tricked the Tunicas into giving them refuge, then repaid their hosts by attacking them in their sleep and plundering their village. News of this misfortune stunned and saddened the French, who had good reason to regard the Tunicas as devoted allies. Another large force converged on the ramshackle fort at Natchitoches, where the garrison comprised no more than twenty men. The commandant, St. Denis, applied to New Orleans for help, and Périer responded by sending out forty men, again under the command of Louboey. Worn out from the previous campaign, Louboey would gladly have relinquished the command to the far more energetic Chevalier de Noyan, Bienville's nephew, who had recently been reinstated as a captain in the Louisiana troops, but Périer refused to make the change. Where Bienville's relations were concerned, he was obviously not as even-handed as he liked to proclaim. In any event, before the army reached Natchitoches, word reached Louboey that St. Denis had managed to repel the Natchez with the help of the neighboring Indians and a few Spaniards. Louboey immediately turned back, without making any attempt to intercept the fleeing Natchez, which he could easily have done.

For the next year or two, bands of Natchez continued to harass the French on the Mississippi and in the settlements. Some of them also prowled around their old home where Baron de Cresnay and eighty soldiers, together with several slaves were preparing to erect a new fort on the ruins of Fort Rosalie. Pretending to be desirous of making peace with the French, they asked to be allowed into the fort and Cresnay, who knew nothing about native tactics, was persuaded of their good intentions. The upshot was that he allowed them into the fort where another battle ensued which cost several lives on both sides. Despite these sporadic assaults, the war had taken a terrible toll on the Natchez. In a few years, all that remained of the once powerful nation were a few small bands who roamed the swamps and bayous bordering the Black River, and another group who took refuge with the Chickasaws.

The prisoners taken in the siege of the Black River camp were spared, as Périer had promised, but they were sent to Saint-Domingue to be sold as slaves, a miserable fate for freedom-loving Indians.

The Natchez War brought an end to Company rule in Louisiana. Unable to carry the financial burden any longer, the Company ceded the colony to the king in late 1730. The following spring Edme Salmon was sent out to replace La Chaise, who had died the previous year. Actually the Company had been disillusioned with La Chaise for some time. After his early spurt of activity, he had done very little to clear up the backlog of accounts, while devoting much of his time to his two habitations, which as finance officer for the Company he was forbidden to own. And if further proof be needed of the depths to which their former star had fallen, the Company had appointed previous director Delorme to take his place—the same Delorme whom La Chaise had once denounced so vigorously—but Delorme died before reaching Louisiana. Périer was kept on, with the title of governor now that Louisiana was a royal province, but not for long. As the full story of the Natchez War became known, he came under increasing fire for his handling of the uprising, and especially for having appointed Detchéparre as commandant. Lengthy diatribes about the unfortunate governor poured into the navy ministry. Dartaguiette criticized him for his mismanagement of the Choctaws; Major Beauchamp blamed him for his ineptitude in Indian affairs generally, and Engineer Broutin faulted him for giving too much authority to his good friend Jean Baron, who was not an engineer at all. According to Broutin, it was Baron who was responsible for the botched siege works at the Natchez post. To add insult to injury, Baron himself blamed his former patron and friend for the "dishonorable" peace with the Natchez. The wrath of the French controller general Phillibert d'Orry also came down on Périer's head about "the so-called siege of the Natchez" and the wanton destruction of the Chaouache nation. "I even see," he continued "that you propose to destroy the other small nations from the sea as far as New Orleans. . . . That is a thing to which I absolutely cannot give my consent, for that is to act against all the rules of statecraft and humanity."[3] He even went so far as to accuse Périer of dereliction of duty.

[3]Orry to Perier, November 1, 1730, *MPA*, 4:25-32.

Instead of visiting the posts as he had been instructed to do, Orry contended, Périer stayed in New Orleans to tend to his own plantation; and there were hints that the governor was profiting from illegal trading carried on by his personal chaplain. The message was brutally clear: Périer was placing his own interests above the good of the colony. Count Maurepas, though less harsh in his condemnation, also criticized Périer's treatment of the Indians, and denounced the commandant's decision to deport the Natchez prisoners, fearing that it would turn the other nations against the French.

The more Périer was held responsible for the crisis in Indian relations, the louder rose the call for Bienville's return. On February 2, 1732, Bienville was summoned from his enforced retirement to become governor of Louisiana. As the king's instructions explained:

> In this crisis his Majesty has thought that he could do nothing more advantageous for this colony than to entrust its government to the care of Sieur de Bienville who . . . has given indication of his experience and his capacity, and he has the more gladly decided to make this choice because he knows that Sieur de Bienville possesses the confidence of the settlers and that of the Indians.[4]

[4]King to Bienville, February 2, 1732, *MPA*, 3:541.

Chapter XI
Bienville Returns

In early December 1732, Bienville set sail from Rochefort on the *Garonne*. The 52-day voyage with nothing to do except wait for the ship to dock afforded him ample time for reflection about the situation he was facing in Louisiana. The Natchez massacre, together with the human tragedy and financial losses it entailed, was a grim warning that there might be no colony unless he took decisive measures before it was too late. Everywhere along the frontier between Louisiana and Carolina, the English were winning over the native tribes, even those who were once so loyal to France; yet the king was confident that Bienville would soon reverse the trend—at the same time as His Majesty was cutting down on the Indian gift fund. As for the troublesome Chickasaws, Bienville was authorized to handle them as he deemed fit. If they could be persuaded to stop harboring the remaining Natchez and cease their own efforts to detach other tribes from the French alliance, so much the better. If not, he was authorized to force them into submission. Obviously Bienville would need all the Le Moyne toughness and diplomacy, and a certain amount of good luck, in the days ahead.

The *Garonne* arrived in Cap Français towards the end of January 1733. When Bienville stepped ashore, he encountered a few Natchez chiefs now enslaved on the island who were hoping to be allowed to return with him to Louisiana. Their spokesman St. Cosme told him that there had been no general conspiracy against the French; the Natchez themselves had been driven to revolt because of the harsh treatment that had been meted out to them by the French. If their story was true, as Bienville hoped, it would make his job easier, for the Chickasaws might be more amenable to his peace efforts. Meanwhile, prudence demanded that he investigate for himself before admitting potential trouble-makers.

If Périer is to be believed, Bienville's behavior on his arrival in New Orleans left much to be desired. No doubt the ill-will shown to him by Company officials still rankled. Now that fortune was smiling on the new governor, it was Périer's turn to squirm. Basking in the glow of ministerial approval, Bienville treated his predecessor with ill-concealed contempt. He dispatched Major Macarty, the adjutant of New Orleans to the outgoing governor, ordering him to remove his furniture from Bienville's house immediately. For good measure, Macarty, who was apparently drunk, added a few choice words of his own—all of which so affronted Périer that he refused to have anything more to do with Bienville. Périer immediately fired off a letter to Maurepas, contrasting his own magnanimous treatment of Bienville's relatives to the disrespect now being visited on him. Seeing that Chateauguay, the Noyans, and Boisbriant had all been stripped of their ranks and disgraced, one wonders how Périer could make that claim.

The general public greeted Bienville's arrival "with unparalleled expressions of joy." By then they were heartily tired of the Périer regime. The governor had the bad luck of being in power during the only serious assault on the colony, and he was held to blame for all the havoc that ensued. In the circumstances, it is not surprising that the settlers welcomed back a leader with a proven record in Indian diplomacy.

Bienville had little time for rejoicing. His first dispatches to the minister presented a thoroughly gloomy picture of the colony. Of course incoming governors usually found it politically expedient to depict the situation they inherited in a bad light in order to make their own achievements look better, but in this case there is good corroborating evidence for his appraisal. Henry de Louboey, an avowed Périer partisan, was writing in May of the same year:

> Every kind of provision is lacking, and we are on the verge of dying of hunger if any accident should happen to the *Ste. Anne*. The colonists are obliged to send their negroes into the woods to gather cane seed to keep them from perishing, and as an additional bit of bad fortune we have seen no money for six months. The salaries of the officers have not been paid. All work has ceased; this puts a number of laborers out of work who do not know what will become of them.[1]

Bienville also found that the population had decreased during the seven-year interim partly because of the Natchez War and partly because several servants and skilled workmen formerly employed by the Company had returned to France after the retrocession. Others had slipped away to the Spanish or English colonies when they found themselves without employment because there was no money to pay them.

When Bienville had a chance to survey the Indian situation, he must have thrown up his hands in despair. Never in the colony's history had French-Indian relations been so poor. All the nations had conceived a "sovereign contempt" for the French, he told the minister, and they "considered as tribute the presents which the King is so kind as to give them." On the other hand, the English had made such progress among them that the Chickasaws entirely belonged to them, some of the Choctaws were wavering, and the Alabamans were inclining in their direction. Even the Illinois were picking groundless quarrels with the French, at the instigation of the English.

[1]Louboey to Maurepas, May 20, 1733, *MPA*, 1:218.

Bienville was particularly worried about the disposition of the Choctaws, for without them on his side, the French would have no allies worth speaking of. Should they defect, or even worse, join with the Chickasaws and their allies to make war on the French, Louisiana would be lost. The Choctaws had good reason to be dissatisfied. They had received only grudging thanks for their support in the Natchez War, and now they were short of everything—hatchets, axes, guns, powder, and the limbourg cloth they liked so much. Since there was nothing Bienville could do until a supply ship arrived from France, he had to postpone a meeting which the chiefs were requesting. Apparently there was more than one way to get limbourg cloth: English smuggling vessels were slipping into Mobile Bay and selling the cloth to the French. Bienville put his foot down on these dealings at once. What would the Choctaws think, he asked, if they saw the French dealing with the English, while forbidding their allies to do the same? A new practice that had crept in during his absence was also disturbing. Instead of giving a large annual present to the Great Chief of the Choctaws, as he himself had been in the habit of doing, and having the chief distribute the contents at his discretion, the Périer administration had been handing out presents to individual chiefs, whose number had swelled to 110. As a result, these chiefs had no incentive to follow the Great Chief, thus fracturing the nation into little fiefdoms who made war or peace when they pleased.

Throughout the spring and summer, Bienville canvassed all his reliable sources about Indian sentiments. For information about the Choctaws, he relied heavily on Father Beaudouin, a Jesuit priest who had spent four years with the nation and knew their language perfectly. Father Beaudouin was the answer to a harried governor's prayer. A consummate diplomat, he knew all the ins and outs of native politics, who were the influential chiefs and who were mere figureheads, and best of all, as Bienville said, he could be trusted because he had no axe to grind.

Bienville's first meeting with the Choctaws gave some grounds for optimism. To be sure the English were still trying to seduce the nation with their cheap and abundant trade goods, and as often as not the Choctaws received them. For all that, Bienville still believed that most of the Choctaws were favorably inclined to the French. They even began to show signs of their willingness to strike at the Chickasaws, who had been making sporadic attacks on *voyageurs*, settlers, and native people. The Choctaw show of support for the French had its effect on their enemies, so that peace feelers began to arrive from some Chickasaw tribes, giving Bienville grounds to believe that those "proud and haughty" warriors were growing weary of war. A few more Choctaw raids on Chickasaw villages might be enough to bring an end to the strife, without having to put a

French army in the field. As he was well aware, short, swift guerilla attacks were far less risky than European-style campaigns.

Unfortunately the first assault on the Chickasaws was a fiasco. In September 1733, close to 600 Choctaws led by Le Sueur, left Mobile to march on Chickasaw country. In spite of a lot of pressure from Diron Dartaguiette who kept pushing for a full-scale French offensive, Bienville refused to commit more than thirty men to the enterprise, being far too cautious to involve a large army in what could well be a defeat which would bring the French into more disrepute among the Indians. It was just as well that he held back. As the army neared the first Chickasaw village, Le Sueur's scouts reported that the Chickasaws were well supplied with English arms and ammunition. Before long most of the attackers melted away, leaving Le Sueur, the Choctaw chief known to the French as Red Shoe, and a few stragglers to face what might come. Deciding that an attack would be futile, the two leaders also turned back.

Meanwhile the English tried their hands at negotiating a peace between the Choctaws and the Chickasaws. To sweeten the deal, they offered the natives three times as much for their pelts as the Choctaws could obtain from the French. They also spread rumors of an imminent English-French war in Europe which they predicted the English were sure to win, after which the French would be chased out of Louisiana. Several chiefs, including Red Shoe, were seduced into going to Carolina for the cheap goods. When they arrived, their reception left something to be desired, and Red Shoe rather shamefacedly returned to the French fold, but not before he had made a trip to the new territory of Georgia to negotiate with the Georgia traders.

With all his painstaking attention to Indian affairs, Bienville also had a colony to run. For once in his life he had a financial officer, Edme Salmon, with whom he was able to work in harmony. Immediately after his arrival, the governor set to work to get the army in shape. One by one, he reviewed the officers and appointed replacements for vacant positions, subject of course to the minister's approval; and he took special care to appoint post commanders who were prudent, intelligent, and above all respected by the Indians. A few of the new cadets were unlikely to strike terror into the hearts of the enemy. A Louboey protégé who had lost his parents in the Natchez War was only eleven years old, and a recent arrival from France was a mere child of five. The latter's death spared Bienville the trouble of having to reject him, but Louboey was so annoyed at having his own candidate rejected that he complained to Maurepas. As usual the soldiers were short of everything: training, food, weapons, even clothing. Bienville was acutely sensitive to the soldiers' living conditions. The men were still lodged in barracks made of piles driven into the ground, covered with "wretched bark of trees on the verge of falling off," without floors, without chimneys, and consequently in continual humidity so that they were often ill. Maurepas finally opened the purse strings, and new barracks in two separate buildings flanking the present Jackson Square were finally under construction in September 1734. A sturdy brick powder magazine to replace an old frame structure constantly subject to flooding was completed in 1736.

There were numerous other needs that had to be filled by a cheese-paring French government. Until 1734 when the new hospital was completed, the sick were housed in a small wooden structure and the sum allotted to maintain it was far too little to accommodate them. Even by the abysmal standards of the day, the furnishings and equipment were pitiable—damaged straw mattresses, torn mosquito nets, broken axes, and even a worn-out tomahawk are among the items listed. Bienville and Salmon painted a grim picture for the minister:

> If your Lordship will be so good as to notice that the King maintains eight hundred troops in the colony and that half and often two thirds of those troops suffer every year from fever and dysentery which oblige us to admit them to the hospital, you will see that 5000 livres is not nearly enough to treat so many patients. We are not including in this many unfortunate inhabitants exhausted by hardship whom charity does not permit us to abandon.[2]

In a few years the poor unfortunates in question had reason to be thankful for the charity of a bachelor trader named Jean Louis who left the bulk of his estate—10,000 *livres* in all—to endow a charity hospital. This little windfall enabled Bienville and Salmon to buy a house and begin taking in a few derelicts. Meanwhile, the Ursuline nuns took charge of the main hospital, which also did duty as a convent building.

These nuns who were such an asset to Louisiana had also fallen on hard times. They came to the colony in 1727 primarily to look after the hospital, but also to set up a school. While they were waiting for the hospital to be ready, they got busy with their educational work. Within a year they had twenty boarders and several day pupils, and what was more surprising for that day and age, a sprinkling of boarders and day girls were Blacks and Indians. Out of charity, the sisters also took in some orphan children, and before long they were looking after many more who had lost their parents in the Natchez War. Stingy as the Company of the Indies had been, it had paid the nuns 150 *livres* a year for each orphan's room and

[2]Bienville and Salmon to Maurepas, May 12, 1733, *MPA*, 3:606-7.

board, as well as paying the rent for the convent itself. After the retrocession, the Crown cut down on the subsidy and refused to pay the rent on the house. As a result, the rent was more than two years in arrears and the owner, Mrs. Kolly, was threatening to sue. At the intervention of Salmon, strongly endorsed by Bienville, Maurepas reversed himself and the nuns were able to continue their nursing and teaching without being weighed down with financial worries.

The ordinary inhabitants who were so glad to see the end of the Company expected better times under the royal regime, but if anything the situation got worse. With the Company store shut down, they had no outlet for the little produce they had to sell, especially their rice which they had in abundance and which the Company had accepted in part payment of debt. And almost everyone was indebted to the Company, particularly for slaves. Naturally the Company expected to be repaid, a virtual impossibility in an essentially barter society. Foreign trade brought little or nothing into the coffers. The tobacco trade, which had shown such promise before the Natchez War, was in tatters and the cotton trade was in its infancy. Even the buckskin trade had fallen off because of the war; it remained to be seen whether the king's decision to abolish the monopoly and open up the trade to individuals would improve matters. In a business which operated on credit, hardly anyone had the means to invest in trade goods and wait months or years to be reimbursed with pelts. Besides, English blandishments and the everlasting war between the Choctaws and the Chickasaws made trading a risky venture. Still Bienville and Salmon estimated that the trade could bring in 30,000 to 40,000 *livres* a year in normal times. They also predicted that the colony could produce and export tobacco, silk, indigo, cotton, pitch and tar if there were more slaves and skilled workers. But exaggerated reports of the Natchez atrocities discouraged people from emigrating to a country where they might be murdered in their beds; and as for sending negroes, that was an expense the Crown was unwilling to undertake.

Meanwhile, the sentiments of the Choctaws wavered from day to day. The two important chiefs, Red Shoe and Alibama Mingo continued to hedge their bets, now trading with the English, now expressing loyalty to the French. Still Bienville continued to believe that all this flirtation with the English was mainly to pressure the French for better trade terms. Choctaw war parties still harassed the Chickasaws and in September 1734 a large party set out again, partly at the urging of Diron Dartaguiette who was always in favor of large-scale offensives. By his own admission he played on the Choctaws' superstition by pretending to have had a dream "that they would fall into the utmost misfortune if they resorted to the English." With Le Sueur at their head, the Choctaws set off for Chickasaw country to strike another blow at their enemies. On the way, some of them began having bad dreams of their own and the army dispersed. All of this infuriated Bienville who blamed Dartaguiette for his silly "dreaming" and for not going along with the expedition himself. A leader who urged others to go on the attack and stayed home himself did not inspire confidence in the Indians.

For several months, the game of cat and mouse continued. At times it looked as though the Chickasaws were ready to return the Natchez refugees to the French in order to open the door for peace negotiations; at other times the English seemed on the verge of detaching the Choctaws from the French alliance. Each shift in the wind caused Bienville to modify his tactics in the hope of bringing a peaceful end to the conflict. That he was sensitive about how his temporizing tactics might appear to the minister is obvious:

> All the letters that I have had the honor of writing to your Lordship for two years about the government of the Indians, principally of the Choctaw nation appear so full of contradictions that when one compares the different plans that I have set forth in them either to terminate the war with the Chickasaws or to frustrate the measures that the English are taking to win over our nations, one might with some appearance of reason charge me with instability or with irresolution.[3]

His hopes of peace were dashed by an unfortunate incident that took place in 1735. A party of Chickasaws and Natchez on their way to the Illinois country ambushed a French detachment convoying ammunition to the Illinois garrison, killed eight soldiers, and made off with the cargo. Later, a Chickasaw delegation attempted to placate Bienville for what they claimed to be an unplanned attack unsanctioned by the Chickasaw leaders; yet they failed to show their goodwill by surrendering some Natchez prisoners. Behind the scenes, the English did their part to thwart any Chickasaw overture to the French, while redoubling their efforts to win over the Choctaws. By late summer 1735, Bienville came face to face with the fact that he would have to launch a decisive strike against the Chickasaws, or risk the endless ambushes which threatened to paralyse Mississippi traffic and cut off access to the Illinois post. Yet the prospect of a campaign into unknown territory worried him in more ways than one. The Canadian experience had taught him that campaigns into native territories had often come dangerously close to disaster. Moreover, the newly arrived soldiers, all recruited at random in Europe, were unlikely to show up well in

[3]Bienville to Maurepas, February 10, 1736, *MPA*, 1:276-77.

primitive conditions. The Choctaws were also a doubtful proposition. He was never sure from one week to the next how many warriors he could count on to join the campaign, and while he welcomed their support, they could also be difficult to handle. The exact location of the Chickasaw forts and the size of the fighting force were also unknown. All he knew was that the Chickasaws lived on "a large plain divided into seven villages of which five have each a stockade fort and all have several fortified cabins" and that the Natchez refugees had two villages nearby, one of which was also well fortified.

In spite of all his troubling reservations, war preparations continued throughout the winter of 1735. The plan of campaign called for a two-pronged attack on the Chickasaw forts. The northern forces would be led by Pierre Dartaguiette, post commander at Fort Chartres in the Illinois country; and Bienville would lead his troops by way of the Tombigbee River to Fort Tombigbee, a new fort that was being erected on the river. Both forces would rendezvous near the Chickasaw villages in the present Pontotoc County, in northern Mississippi.

Dartaguiette's army of 114 Frenchmen and over 330 Indians left Fort de Chartres in February 1736 and arrived at Fort Prudhomme towards the end of the month. Once there the soldiers constructed a small fort and Dartaguiette dispatched scouts to locate the Chickasaw forts and make contact with Bienville's army. As the days passed and provisions began to run low, his native allies, who were not used to fighting in the winter, grew weary and impatient with the delay. Unable to restrain them any longer, Dartaguiette proceeded across the Indian trail towards the Chickasaw villages in the hope of meeting with Bienville. On March 20, a courier arrived from the governor with word that he would not arrive till the end of April. Meanwhile, Dartaguiette's scouts had located the Chickasaw village of Chocolissa. At a council meeting, the decision was taken to capture the village and plunder it for provisions to feed the already dwindling army. While they were charging against Chocolissa, a large force swooped down upon them from the nearby woods. In the rout which ensued, what remained of Dartaguiette's army was cut to pieces. Dartaguiette himself and a few of his hardiest men, including the Jesuit priest Father Senat, were captured and burned at the stake. Powder, bullets, pack horses, and, worst of all, Bienville's dispatches containing the plan of campaign, later translated by English advisors, all fell into enemy hands.

Back in the colony, the fates were conspiring against Bienville. French vessels were late in arriving, and when they did arrive they had no mortars and not enough provisions for the army. Boats to convey the men upriver which were supposed to be ready in October were still unfinished in mid-January, so Bienville had to rush back from Mobile to New Orleans to hurry things up. Finally, on April 1, the 600-man army consisting of officers, regular troops, militia, and black slaves led by free blacks, set out from Mobile. Buffeted by rains and gales, the boats took three weeks to reach Fort Tombigbee and lost half their cargo of rice on the way. There they disembarked and picked up fresh provisions, while Bienville awaited the arrival of the Choctaws who had promised to join him there. After a further delay for speeches and gift-giving, the army continued on its way.

On May 24, the army now well over 1,000 strong, encamped near the Chickasaw village of Ackia. Bienville's orders were to begin by attacking the Natchez villages, which were situated a little to the side of the main Chickasaw village. Through a ruse, Red Shoe convinced him to attack the main village at once. The village consisted of three buildings roofed in clay and surrounded by a double stockade, one of the buildings flying an English flag, and English traders inside to advise the Chickasaws.

At 3 o'clock in the afternoon of May 26, the Battle of Ackia began. Unknown to Bienville, of course, the Chickasaws were aware of his plans and had stationed 500 warriors in the nearby hills. One hundred men headed by Pierre-Benoît Payen de Noyan led off the French attack by capturing a few small fortified cabins, after which they were met with a hail of fire from loopholes strategically placed in the stockade. Meanwhile the 500 hidden warriors swooped down from the hills. The French were sitting ducks, unable to defend themselves and unable to penetrate the stockade without cannons or mortars. What followed was another rout.

At five in the evening, Bienville ordered the drummers to beat the retreat. The dejected men marched to the landing place carrying their wounded with them, and boarded the boats for Mobile. On their arrival, they were met with the news of Dartaguiette's defeat and death.

This double defeat was a bitter humiliation for the French, particularly for Bienville who had been sent to Louisiana to restore peace and security to the colony. More than a hundred men had died on the battlefield, including excellent officers such as Pierre Dartaguiette, Joseph de Lusser, and Chevalier de Contrecoeur; and Chevalier de Noyan along with several other officers was gravely wounded. When Maurepas heard about the botched campaign, he excoriated the demoralized governor for his indecision and mismanagement.

To be sure there was blame enough to go around. The late arrival of the French ships delayed Bienville's departure, and the failure to send mortars made it impossible for the French to penetrate the Indian fortifications. Even the elements were against the French. Pierre Dartaguiette could also be blamed for allowing his native allies to attack prematurely, but to expect a patient and orderly action from the Indians after three months on the march was out of the question. Bienville blamed himself for listening to Red Shoe's advice and allowing himself to be maneuvred into attacking the Chickasaw fort first, instead of beginning with the Natchez fort which was not so well fortified. But the greatest misfortune was the discovery of the dispatches, which allowed the Chickasaws to prepare themselves for the attack.

No one felt the blow to French prestige more keenly than Bienville. In his report to the minister, he tried as best he could to justify his conduct of the campaign. As well as citing the series of unfortunate setbacks, he complained about the incompetence, not to say cowardice, of the French troops who took to their heels at the first sign of danger. In his opinion many of them were "wretched blackguards" who could never be whipped into shape. As well, he admitted that he had not foreseen the extraordinarily strong fortifications the Indians had managed to erect. Their cabins were covered with a wall of earth proof against burning arrows and grenades so that nothing but bombs could harm them, he reported.

But all the justifications in the world could not placate Maurepas. The defeat was put down to Bienville's irresolution and bungling management, rather than incompetent troops or natural misfortunes. Obviously another campaign would be necessary to subdue the Chickasaws once and for all, and prevent their English allies from securing a foothold on the Mississippi. Just as important, a victory was necessary to restore French prestige among the Choctaws and other friendly tribes, who might otherwise be tempted to defect.

Chapter XII
The Second Chickasaw War

In the aftermath of the Chickasaw War, Bienville had little to cheer him and much to be concerned about. On the one hand he was convinced of the necessity to chastise the Chickasaws, yet it was obvious that it would take some time before the poor colony was in a position to launch another full-scale offensive. Torn by the prospect of a delay which would allow the enemy to consolidate their position and perhaps encourage his Choctaw allies to defect from the French alliance, he also knew the dangers inherent in a premature attack. To add to his miseries, a bout of painful sciatica kept him in bed when he had myriad tasks to conduct.

After taking stock of the military situation, he dispatched an urgent appeal to Maurepas for effective aid. His experience in the previous campaign had taught him the futility of attacking stockaded villages without artillery or experienced men, so he requested 400 seasoned troops and 250 recruits, a fighting force which he deemed large enough to allow the settlers to stay at home and tend to their crops instead of having to take part in the fighting. In addition, there were requests for the necessary arms supplies, including bombs, mortars, and light cannon.

Naturally Bienville was counting on some support from the Choctaws. Word came to him from Fort Condé that they were still pushing for parity between French and English prices. To keep the warriors on his side, he decided to approve the change, though not immediately, in order to avoid the appearance of weakness. Instead, he decided to wait for the arrival of the king's ships, after which he informed the chiefs that the king was giving them a bonus for their assistance in the previous campaign. He also told the minister that the native warriors could not be expected to feed themselves while they were fighting a French war. They too would need to be supplied with food as well as the usual arms and ammunition.

Initially, he planned to use the route followed in the previous campaign. It was the nearest to the Choctaw villages and the most familiar, but it represented its own problems. During the rainy season, the Tombigbee River was usually flooded, and in dry weather the water subsided so much that it was unsuitable for heavily laden pirogues, besides being so narrow that travelers presented a perfect target for snipers. Consequently, he sent out three parties to explore three possible routes and map out trails and portages. The first expedition under Chief Engineer Ignace Broutin retraced the route taken in the previous campaign; the second, commanded by the engineer Bernard de Vergés, went by way of the Mississippi River to explore the Prudhomme Bluffs-Wolf River approach; and the third headed by Captain Jean-Baptiste de Membrède scouted out a possible route by way of the Yazoo River. After studying the maps of the three routes in June 1738, Bienville and Salmon decided on the Mississippi-Prudhomme Bluffs approach. What tipped the scales was De Vergés' report, based on the assurances of his Arkansas guides, that the departure spot he had chosen from the Mississippi into the interior, the mouth of the St. Francis River, was only twenty leagues from Chickasaw country. In actual fact it was about twice that distance. When the mistake was discovered the following year, the plans were already too far advanced to permit a change.

Meanwhile, with the information gleaned from the 1736 campaign and the reports of scouting parties, draughtsman Alexandre M. de Batz was able to sketch the lay-out of the Chickasaw forts and villages. By another stroke of luck, a Choctaw chief had managed to lay hands on a rough diagram made by a Chickasaw war chief, showing the position of those tribes whom the Chickasaws considered to be friends or foes, as well as the trails used by English traders. From the original sketch written on the back of a deerskin, De Batz drew a map which gave Bienville helpful information about the tribes who might be counted on to side with the Chickasaws.

Further encouraging news came from Father Beaudouin. Persuaded by himself and Joseph Chauvin *dit* De Léry, the Choctaws marched against the Chickasaws, not once but twice. In the first raid in the fall of 1737, they made their way to Ackia, the most southerly of the Chickasaw villages and although they did not actually assault the village, they did destroy the crops. Two months later they marched again and destroyed four forts, killing and capturing numerous livestock. Despite their failure to come to grips with the enemy, the Choctaws were wreaking considerable devastation on the Chickasaws and keeping them from their hunting, their main source of income.

The English colonies now became alarmed. A major source of English strength was their economic and political alliance with the Chickasaws; at all costs, the tribe had to be maintained as a strong fighting force. The Carolinians and their fellow colonists in Georgia rallied to the support of their beleaguered allies with copious supplies of arms and ammunition, at the same time redoubling their efforts to turn the Choctaws and the Alabamans against the French. In the summer of 1738, several traders made their way into Choctaw villages with packhorses laden with cheap merchandise and promises of even better deals to come. Using a clever propaganda move, the traders also spread the word that the French intended to destroy all the Indian nations one by one. They even went so far as to say that Bienville had written to the governor of Carolina, asking him to abandon the Chickasaws to the mercies of the French; and when the Chickasaws were wiped out the two European nations could unite to annihilate all the Indians and take their lands for themselves. By October of the same year, Bienville learned that the English were not only being received in several Choctaw villages, but were deflecting some of the chiefs to their side. Alternatively cajoled and intimidated by the redoubtable Red Shoe, who always had a sharp eye for the main chance, many of the Choctaws agreed to make peace with their old enemies. Even the pro-French chiefs were reluctant to take part in any campaign against the Chickasaws, for fear of reprisals from the Red Shoe faction. This worried Bienville, who feared that the war could not be won without their help. In desperation, he implored the minister to see that the troops sent to the colony would be of better caliber than the pathetic specimens commonly sent to Louisiana.

Maurepas did his best to comply with Bienville's request. By the end of November 1738, more than 450 soldiers "suitable for the country" had arrived in the colony. More French ships sailed up the river to New Orleans in the next few months bringing weapons, ammunition, clothing, and provisions of all kinds for the army. Unfortunately, instead of the light artillery that Bienville and Salmon had requested, the government sent 1,000 pound cannon—ideal for shelling a European walled fortress, but hardly suitable for transportation through swamps and canebreaks.

Meanwhile, in September 1738, Captain Jacques de Coustilhas, Engineer Bernard de Vergés, and Chaplain Father Pierre de Vitry (who kept a factual record of the campaign) set out with a contingent of 150 soldiers to the mouth of the St. Francis River to build a storehouse and construct carts which would haul the artillery and supplies into Chickasaw country. Rowing against the current for 676 miles in the burning sun was a gruelling business for the Coustilhas contingent, especially for the new recruits, who were frequently ill from imbibing too freely from the river water. Even the veteran Captain Coustilhas was stricken and he died shortly after reaching the mouth of the St. Francis. While the men labored to construct the carts and the entrepot, the engineer François Saucier went out to explore the route to the Chickasaw forts, at which point Vergés' miscalculation was discovered. To make matters worse, the land was extremely swampy.

When Bienville heard of these developments, he sent his nephew Captain Pierre-Benoît Payen de Noyan up the Mississippi to find a better launching place on higher ground. By mid August, 1739, De Noyan had selected a spot near the site of the present Memphis, Tennessee, and the stockaded post named Fort Assumption was erected to house the men and materials from St. Francis.

In New Orleans the atmosphere was quite buoyant. Apart from the setback caused by the engineer's blunder, everything appeared to be proceeding on schedule. Arrangements had been made to secure horses and oxen from the Illinois and Natchitoches to haul the heavy artillery inland. A good launching spot had apparently been found, and the troops, ammunition, and provisions would shortly arrive at the new post. It is true that Bienville was still unsure of the exact route to be taken from Fort Assumption to Chickasaw territory, but he was counting on the scouts to find one and on the engineers to make it practicable. Word had also come from Governor Beauharnois of Canada that a promised contingent of 500 French and Indians, commanded by Bienville's nephew, Baron de Longueuil, were preparing to set out for the new fort. If the French ships carrying the remaining troops and supplies arrived more or less on schedule, the whole army would be assembled at Fort Assumption by the end of September, when the terrain would still be dry enough to accommodate the heavy carts. There was also good news from the Choctaw front: the troublesome Red Shoe had made another about face. After being rebuffed by the English, who were perhaps tired of his incessant demands and his turncoat ways, the chief began to rally the Choctaws to the French cause.

Just when things were looking promising there was a hitch. The French ships with the final complement of men and provisions were two months late. So instead of leaving in July as he had planned, Bienville had to postpone his departure until September. This meant that the army would not reach Fort Assumption until November, and the campaign itself would not get under way until December the worst time of the year to lead an army overland. In June 1739, Louboey gave vent to the general frustration:

> It is regrettable that the delay of the ships should come to disturb arrangements that are so advantageous and which seemed to promise us a fortunate campaign . . . ; in the month of December and January these animals [the oxen and horses] will have great difficulty in getting enough to live on, without taking into account the abundant rains and snows that ordinarily fall at that season, which might damage the roads so that they will become impracticable, and that would be extremely bad for us.[1]

Bienville fretted and fumed through the hot months of summer. The Canadian troops had to be notified to delay their departure, but what if the message arrived too late? What if the food ran out? What if the Indian allies grew weary of the delay and returned to their homes?

When the long-awaited vessels arrived in New Orleans, many of the soldiers were so ill that they had to be hospitalized. In a week or two, sixty had died and many more were weak or ill. Bienville finally left New

[1]Louboey to Maurepas, June 3, 1739, *MPA*, 1:398.

Orleans on September 12 with a contingent of a hundred French soldiers, and a few blacks and Indians. Three other convoys had preceded him up the river. The first contingent consisting of three marine companies and about 100 blacks and Indians left on July 24. These were followed two weeks later by four companies of soldiers, sixty members of the Louisiana militia, and a smattering of blacks and Indians. Bringing up the rear was M. Louis de Nouailles d'Ayme, leading a force of three Swiss companies, with some sixty blacks and about twenty Indians. De Nouailles, a navy captain, was to be commander-in-chief of all the forces, although he was expected to take advice from Bienville. In other words, if the campaign was successful he would get most of the glory, and if it failed Bienville would get the blame.

As the sixty-year-old governor and his party made their way up the river, they were battered by rain and high winds. Compounding their misery was the fever which the soldiers had picked up at Saint-Domingue. Before the end of October, 50 soldiers had to be sent back to New Orleans; what was worse, the infection was carried to the forces upriver. The flotilla joined the contingent at the St. Francis River outpost on November 3, and both groups shortly departed for Fort Assumption.

On his arrival, Bienville's worst fears were realized: no feasible route could be found to the Chickasaws' forts. First, he studied the map of a route discovered by engineer Saucier. Alas, the road which would have been very practicable in another season was then so flooded by the overflow of several small rivers swollen by the almost constant rains that they were obliged to have a search made for another. While Broutin the engineer was dispatched to look for something better, Bienville waited as patiently as he could at Fort Assumption with his army of over 1,200 Frenchmen and almost twice as many Indians. By then, illness was spreading through the ranks and provisions were running dangerously low. To maintain his Indian allies together, he participated in all the customary speeches and parleying, although his mind was surely distracted with other things. December passed into January and still no trail was discovered. More than half the oxen and cattle transported from St. Francis were lost in the swamps and the rest were too exhausted to haul heavy wagons, while many of the animals from Natchitoches had gone astray.

On January 11, Broutin and Céleron de Blainville (commander of the Canadian forces in the absence of Longueuil, who was stricken with sciatica) returned to the fort with the word that a good trail had been located only twenty-one leagues away; it was the Memphis, Pontotoc, Mobile trail taken by Pierre Dartaguiette in the previous war. Still trees would have to be felled and swollen bayous crossed to get to the route. With half his men sick and hardly any animals to haul the heavy artillery, most of it rusted by the rain, there was nothing for it but to revise the plan of attack. The tons of artillery lugged hundreds of miles to Fort Assumption would not be used at all.

Meanwhile, there were signs that the Chickasaws would be glad to make peace on the best terms they could get. From Chickasaw warriors captured near Fort Assumption, Bienville learned that the tribe was quite weary of war. Long years of fighting the French and the Choctaws had decimated their ranks and destroyed their homes and their crops. Of the eight fortified forts that the French had observed in the 1736 campaign, only two were still serviceable. Earlier on there had been other overtures from the Chickasaws. A conciliatory message from the Great Chief offered to surrender three French prisoners and stop attacking the French, if Bienville halted his army. Indian tokens of peace—a leaf of corn, tobacco, medicine, and a bearskin, laid in a circle—were also strewn at intervals near the French camp. These symbols, disdained at first, began to look more welcome by the day.

In the dilemma in which he found himself, Bienville began to think that it might be advisable to act on the proposals, but not before launching a sudden blow against one of the enemy forts. On February 6, he ordered Céleron to march on the Chickasaw encampment with 180 volunteers and 400 Indians. Within ten days the little army arrived at the fort and began the attack. After a series of minor skirmishes, the Chickasaws sent out twenty warriors with a white flag, but Céleron's Indian allies fired on them. A second time the move was repeated. Further sporadic fighting continued for three days, before Céleron managed to convince his Indian allies to hold their fire until he heard what the Chickasaw delegation had to say. On their arrival in the French camp, the Chickasaw deputies handed over three Natchez to Céleron, protesting that there were only a few of that tribe still among them, after which they promised to surrender the remaining Natchez to Bienville, if the French would call off the siege. Céleron consented and returned to Fort Assumption to make his report.

The day designated for the arrival of the Chickasaws came and went, but no emissaries put in an appearance at Fort Assumption. (It later appeared that the delegation had to turn back three times because of hostile attacks.) By then, the Canadians and most of the Indians had departed for home. All that remained of the regular troops were 500 men, many of them sick. At the end of March the French broke camp and Nouailles and the marine troops returned to New Orleans. While the remaining soldiers were preparing to destroy Fort Assumption, seven of the eleven Chickasaw chiefs appeared bringing with them one lone Natchez woman and three children. By their own account, most of the Natchez had fled to the Cherokees, and any that attempted to return would be exterminated if Bienville promised to restrain the northern tribes and the tribes along the Mississippi River from making any more attacks on them. Bienville agreed, but he made it clear that he could not promise to call off the Choctaws until the latter had received satisfaction for past grievances. After dispensing a few presents to ratify the agreement, he set out for New Orleans.

It need hardly be said that Bienville's prestige was badly eroded by this campaign. It was not the rout of 1736, but it had failed to accomplish its mission. After three years of planning and an investment of about one million *livres* in men and equipment, the war had been abandoned almost without striking a blow. True, seven of the eleven Chickasaw villages had sent their envoys to sue for peace and had acceded to Bienville's conditions, but it was a shabby peace patched up at the last minute, without any real guarantee of success. The fact remained that the enemy had not been annihilated, and if the past was anything to go by, the Chickasaws were unlikely to keep the peace a day longer than suited their convenience, particularly with the English doing all in their power to egg them on.

Although he tried to put the best face on the situation, Bienville's health and self-confidence were seriously undermined. So much so that he was writing to Maurepas in June 1740:

> The labors, the anxieties, and the mental strain that I have had to sustain since it pleased your lordship eight years ago to propose me for this governship have impaired my health to such an extent that I should not have hesitated to entreat you to grant me a leave of absence to go to France by the first royal vessel if the interest of the colony and that of my honor did not demand of me that I put the last touches to the treaty of peace that I entered into with the Chickasaws and the conclusion of which I do not think it advisable to press in order to let the Choctaws have time to avenge on the Chickasaws and on their protectors the insult they have received of them.[2]

He had no delusions about what Maurepas' reaction would be:

> I feel with pain that my lord will be little satisfied with the success of this enterprise which has caused the King such great expense, but I flatter myself at the same time that he will be so good as to observe that I had not failed to take any of the precautions necessary in order to render this campaign as glorious as His Majesty had reason to expect.[3]

It was not very long before the minister was hearing a different story from other sources. On his return to France, Noailles cast all the blame for

[2]Bienville to Maurepas, June 18, 1740, *MPA*, 3:738.

[3]Bienville to Maurepas, May 6, 1740, *MPA*, 1:459.

the faulty campaign on the governor, although he himself had been more of a nuisance than a help throughout. Critics in the colony took pen to paper to voice their criticism to the minister—and of course to justify their own part in the affair. Salmon complained that the expedition caused "much damage to the colony and much expense to the King" without any assurance of peace. Engineer Vergés, who was as much to blame as anyone for the outcome, complained of the bickering between Bienville, Noailles, and the other officers. Even allowing for the fact that some of the criticism was ill-advised or based on misinformation, the fact remained that Bienville was the governor and he had to accept responsibility for the overall plan. That an army so out of proportion to the enemies' resources should have come so far and done so little was not something any commander could be proud of. It could be argued that the whole undertaking was far too ambitious for a sprawling country with no roads and slow communication. Also, Bienville's respect for the Chickasaw fighting spirit might have made him too slow and too cautious. The presence of Nouailles, who made up for his own ignorance of wilderness warfare by constant carping, did not help matters. But when all this has been said, what the governor lacked above all was the element of good luck. The late arrival of the French forces delayed the campaign which he had planned for the usually favorable autumn weather. Moreover, if the troops had arrived in March, they would probably have been spared the illness which normally struck Saint-Domingue only in the summer. The error made by Engineer Vergés slowed matters still further. And one may well ask why the French sent 1,000-pound cannons to a country where the distances were so great and roads non-existent. This alone, together with the loss of the horses and oxen, made a large scale offensive into enemy territory impossible.

Despite everything, the flawed campaign did have some positive results for Louisiana. Even if the Chickasaws had not been defeated, their fangs were drawn and they were no longer much of a threat to the colony. The massive show of force on the part of the French also worried the English, who feared that Louisiana might strike again to annihilate the Chickasaws. With the Chickasaws spent as a fighting force, Louisiana and its native allies could pose a serious threat to South Carolina, perhaps attack Charles Town itself. For fear of just such an assault, it was thought advisable for English traders to lie low for a while and stay closer to home. Moreover, the Carolinians had trouble in their own backyard at the time. The black slaves who outnumbered the white population by about 40,000 to 25,000, were becoming increasingly unhappy with their wretched lot and actually staged a brief uprising in 1739; and the following year the Carolinians suffered a humiliating setback of their own when they attempted to capture the Spanish fort at St. Augustine.

As for the Chickasaws, with the exception of a few minor incidents, they kept to the terms of the treaty. The Choctaws, who were not bound by the agreement, felt free to settle scores with their enemies over old and new wrongs. Bienville himself had no illusions that the accord was perfect. He was writing in 1741:

> As for the solidity of the peace with the Chickasaws, I have always thought and I have written in the same sense to your Lordship that it [the peace] would be as good as it could be on the word of Indians but that it was not possible to count on it absolutely.[4]

Nonetheless, for the time being, the French could breathe easier.

With the end of the war, the deerskin trade began to revive, especially at Fort Tombigbee. Founded as a base for the first Chickasaw campaign, the new post was a strategic place for monitoring the politics of the Choctaws, as well as the focal point of the trade. Other trade was slowly picking up as well, partly as a result of a French edict that abolished taxes on certain goods traded with Martinique, Saint-Domingue, and the other French islands in the West Indies. In February 1743 Bienville was writing quite optimistically:

> The commerce between the islands and the colony is increasing every day. Last year more than 12 boats came laden with wine, flour, and rum and for this merchandise they carried away building timber, planks, rice, peas and beans. The return cargoes from France would increase still more if the inhabitants had as much strength as good will. The trade in deerskins amounts at present to more than one hundred thousand pounds, pitch and tar to more than we hoped for, and indigo will yield as much as the American islands since we have made more than three cuttings this year which have yielded abundantly in proportion to the small quantity of negroes who have been employed on this crop.[5]

A beginning was also made on the production of myrtle wax which was to become an important product by the end of the decade. The wax myrtle was particularly abundant around Mobile and the inhabitants were beginning to extract the wax for their own candles. Nine years later, the successful planter Chevalier de Pradel was writing that he had sold part of his crop for 3,000 *livres* and still had the greater part in his barn.

[4]Bienville to Maurepas, April 30, 1741, *MPA*, 3:747.

[5]Bienville to Maurepas, February 4, 1743, *MPA*, 3:776-77.

Both Bienville and Salmon were concerned about the lack of educational facilities for boys. The little school set up by Father Raphael in 1725 closed with the departure of the Company of the Indies. Father Beaubois had hopes of establishing a Jesuit school, but his dream was not realized. It was time to bring up the subject again. In a dispatch to the minister, Bienville and Salmon emphasized that a Jesuit school was a necessity for many reasons, not the least of which was to put a stop to the practice of sending young men from well-to-do families to France to be educated. They feared that most of these young men might become "disgusted" with Louisiana and return to it only to collect the heritage left to them by their parents. Obviously Bienville was the one who wanted the Jesuits, for the very next day Salmon wrote a private letter to Maurepas, asking for Christian Brothers, who would do the job for less money. Bienville was long gone before any school was founded.

The aging governor got a lift of excitement when two *coureurs de bois*, Paul and Pierre Mallet, appeared in New Orleans with an amazing story to tell. On their own, without backing or advice from anyone, they had gone all the way from Fort Chartres in Illinois country to Santa Fe, New Mexico, where they were wined and dined by the Spanish governor, Gaspar Domingo de Mendoza, pending instructions from the viceroy in Mexico City about what should be done about them. The long wait gave the two men a chance to talk to travellers and figure out a possible route from Santa Fe to New Orleans. On May 1, 1740, they left Santa Fe and made their way to the Canadian River, which has been named after them, until they came to the Arkansas, after which they floated down to the Mississippi and on to the capital to tell Bienville about their discovery. From his first arrival in Louisiana, Bienville had had a hankering to discover the elusive route, and the Company of the Indies had spent a lot of money outfitting explorers to find one, but without success. With something of his old enthusiasm, Bienville told the minister about the surprising new discovery and the possibilities of future trade which it opened up. While he was awaiting a reply, he took it upon himself to send the Mallets back to retrace their steps. However, on the second journey the Canadian River was too shallow to float the canoes and the Mallets returned to the Illinois. It would be nine more years before they set out for Santa Fe again. By then, Bienville was back in France.

The years of toil and frustration were beginning to take their toll. In a poignant letter to Maurepas written in May 1742, Bienville asked for his recall:

> If success had always responded to my application to the affairs of this government, I should gladly have devoted the rest of my life to it, but a sort of fatality bent for some time upon frustrating the majority of my

> best concerted plans has often made me lose the fruit of my labors and perhaps a part of your Lordship's confidence. I have therefore thought that I should not resist my bad fortune any longer. I hope that the officer who will be chosen to replace me will be more fortunate than I. I am going to devote all my attention during the rest of the time that I shall spend here to smooth out as far as will be possible for me to do so the difficulties attached to the position that I shall hand over and I can flatter myself that I shall leave affairs to him in better order than they have ever been.[6]

The man chosen to replace him was Pierre de Rigaud, Marquis de Vaudreuil, the former governor of Trois Rivières, Quebec, and the son of a former governor general of Canada. Vaudreuil arrived in New Orleans on July 21, 1743. In the usual tradition, the new governor painted a gloomier picture of Louisiana than the facts supported, no doubt hoping to make the immensity of the task with which he was faced appear all the greater. However, he assured Maurepas in rather grandly sweeping terms, he would eventually bring order and tranquillity to the troubled colony. Yet, as time went on his policies were remarkably in tune with those of his predecessor.

Bienville departed New Orleans on August 17, 1743, and arrived in Rochefort two months later. Regrettably, contemporary accounts are silent about the farewell the colonists accorded to the man who had guided Louisiana through its worst years.

[6]Bienville to Maurepas, March 26, 1742, *MPA*, 3:763-64.

Chapter XIII
Bienville's Last Years

Bienville spent his final years in Paris in an apartment on the Rue Vivienne in a building which still stands today. The proceeds from his French investments and his Louisiana properties enabled the retired bachelor to live in comfort. He had a carriage and horses to convey him to visit old friends and relatives, a valet and a footman to attend to his personal needs, and a cook, a kitchen maid, and a coachman. According to an inventory taken after his death, his lodgings consisted of his own large bedroom and two smaller bedrooms next to the kitchen for the servants, a salon containing the usual furnishings with a carpet somewhat the worse for wear, two smaller rooms and a well-stocked wine cellar. An attached stable housed his carriage and two black horses.

His last will and testament drawn up on January 15, 1765, is very much what one would expect from a man who was extremely attached to his family and kind to the poor. After making provision for masses for the repose of his soul, he bequeathed legacies to all his servants and a gift of 1,000 pounds to the poor of the parish. The bulk of his estate was left to the descendants of his three brothers, Longueuil, Sérigny, and Chateauguay, while other relatives each received the gift of a diamond.[1]

The bitterest disappointment for the aging ex-governor must have been the passing of Canada and Louisiana into foreign hands. After the prolonged struggle known in Europe as the Seven Years War and in North America as the French and Indian War, the tides of war had turned against France. On September 8, 1760, the Cross of St. George replaced the *fleur-de-lis* over the ramparts of Montreal, marking the end of French rule in the land for which so many of Bienville's family and relatives had fought, and worked, and died. The Treaty of Paris which ended the war also awarded Florida and all of Louisiana east of the Mississippi, except the port of New Orleans, to the English. As well, in a secret agreement between France and Spain signed in November 1762, King Louis XV ceded to his cousin of Spain "from the pure impulse of his generous heart" all the remaining Louisiana territory. Officially, French rule in Louisiana was at an end.

On October 20, 1763, the music of bagpipes greeted the hoisting of the British flag over Fort Condé, renamed Fort Charlotte after the British queen. The French regiment and a sprinkling of inhabitants withdrew to New Orleans, but the majority took the requisite oath of allegiance to their new ruler and remained in their old homes. Shortly afterwards, Fort Toulouse and Fort Tombigbee also changed hands and Fort Chartres in Illinois

[1]For a copy of the will, see the Appendix.

country was handed over in 1765. With this, the British occupation was virtually complete.

The Spanish occupation did not proceed quite so smoothly. It was not until September 1764 that the then governor, Jean-Jacques D'Abbadie, received official word of the secret Franco-Spanish agreement. To their dismay, the colonists learned that they were being abandoned by their king and expected to bow the knee to Charles III of Spain. A mass meeting was held in New Orleans at which it was decided to send a delegation led by a prominent settler, Jean Milhet, to France to beg King Louis XV not to relinquish Louisiana. The king did not meet the delegation, but tradition has it that Bienville managed to arrange an interview with the prime minister, the Duc de Choiseul, who listened politely to their pleas but promised nothing.

Spain was in no hurry to take over its vast new possession, perhaps leading Bienville to hope that there might be no secession after all. Any hopes that the arrangement might only be temporary were shortly dashed. Abbadie died in 1765 and was succeeded by Charles-Philippe Aubry. Later that year, a letter arrived from Don Antonio de Ulloa announcing his imminent arrival to take over the reins of government. Eight months later Ulloa disembarked at New Orleans. With only seventy men and faced with a sullen population, the new governor was unable to take effective control over the colony. His only recourse was to keep the French administration in place until a larger contingent of Spanish reinforcements arrived to take charge of the posts. So Governor Aubry was in the peculiar position of commanding for the king of France and governing for the king of Spain. French ships continued to sail up the Mississippi and French merchants kept the colony supplied with goods.

Finally, Spain sprang into action. A decree of October 1768 stipulated that only Spanish ships could enter the harbor and all trade would be carried on only with Spanish merchants. The simmering discontent immediately boiled over. Egged on by Commissary Denis-Nicolas Foucault and Nicolas Chauvin de Lafrénière, the attorney general, as well as several leading merchants, a plot was hatched to expel Ulloa from Louisiana. On the morning of October 28, the conspirators entered New Orleans and forced Ulloa and his retinue to sail to Havana.

Spain's reaction was swift and sure. Nine months later a large flotilla carrying 3,000 crack soldiers commanded by Gen. Alejandro O'Reilly came to restore order in the colony and punish the ringleaders of the insurrection. Twelve of the leaders including Bienville's two grandnephews, Jean-Baptiste de Noyan and Bienville de Noyan were arrested and charged with high treason. Six of these, including Jean-Baptiste de Noyan, paid with their lives for their attachment to France.

Very soon, order was restored and O'Reilly returned to Spain. The new governor, Luis de Unzaga ruled with a light hand. By appointing French colonists to the Cabildo, which replaced the Superior Council, and retaining French as Indian agents, he managed to gain the loyalty of the people. Better still, taxes were kept low and, at long last, Louisiana gained access to lucrative Spanish markets in the New World.

Bienville had been dead for more than a year before his beloved colony effectively passed into Spanish hands. On March 7, 1767, after an illness of two months, the last survivor of the Le Moyne brothers ended a long life filled with achievements and frustrations.

Chapter XIV
Conclusion

Like the Mississippi River itself, Bienville's career had many unexpected twists and turns. He came to Louisiana as Iberville's faithful lieutenant, adventurous and resourceful to be sure, but a lieutenant nonetheless, whose function it was to carry out the policies of his older brother. Iberville's untimely illness and eventual death changed everything. Catapulted into a leadership role at the age of 22, Bienville performed prodigies to stave off attacks and avert the total collapse of the infant colony. Year in year out, he held off the encroaching English, kept a wary eye on his jealous Spanish neighbors, patched and repatched his network of Indian alliances, borrowed food from Pensacola in times of hunger, and juggled funds around to make ends meet. Yet instead of receiving the rewards he believed to be his due, he incurred the wrath of the home government. With the appointment of Governor de Muy, he was shuffled to the sidelines for good, or so it was intended. But De Muy's death and the ineptitude of two succeeding governors, Cadillac and Lépinay, again thrust him on center stage until he eventually became commandant general in name as well as in fact after nineteen years of continuous service. Swept out of office seven years later as a result of the disorders surrounding Law's efforts at colonization, he was consigned to seven years of obscurity in France before being called back to rescue an imperilled colony. But he could not work miracles. Worn out with his exertions, he no longer had the vigor and optimism characteristic of his earlier career. At the age of sixty-two, he was ready to hand over the reins to a younger man.

Any assessment of Bienville's career must take the evidence of his arbitrary ways into account. Even allowing for the fact that Louisiana history is littered with records of the quarrels and back-stabbing of its officials, it cannot be denied that Bienville had a special knack for making enemies for himself. To some extent the early clashes could be excused. Bienville was a young man burdened with enormous responsibilities in a colony chronically short of the bare necessities of life. The settlers—for the most part, fractious, hard-drinking soldiers and rowdy Canadians—were enough to try any leader's patience even at the best of times. And if he was inflexible in his dealings with his two major opponents, Father de La Vente and Nicolas de La Salle, the two men were equally unbending. What Bienville lacked at this stage of his career was a trusted advisor, older in years and experience, who might have taught him to be more circumspect. Indeed, it may well be that open disputes would have been avoided had the Jesuits been placed in charge of the Louisiana mission, because Bienville heeded the Jesuits as he did no one else. As it was, however, he continued to allow his contentiousness to get in the way of his own self-interest. The long years of slights and disappointments did nothing to improve Bienville's temper. Feuds continued to develop with commissioners, directors, and other Company employees. They resented him for his despotic ways and he complained that these newcomers who knew nothing at all about the country opposed him at every turn. Predictably, his opponents made their feelings known to the Company, often in the hope of gaining advantages for themselves, while he himself had no patron in high places to shield him from his political enemies. During his last ten years in Louisiana, Bienville's relationship with his associates was generally good and he deserves as much credit as anyone for this. Of course he was no longer saddled with a motley collection of Company commissioners and directors, here one year, gone the next, always looking over his shoulder, with the superiority of the Frenchman for the colonial. And as a governor and one who enjoyed the support of the navy minister, the ground was firmer under his feet, so he no longer felt the need to assert himself. Except for one brief dispute, his relations with Salmon were without serious incident, and even that disagreement was shortly patched up.

In the final analysis, the constant bickering probably had more to do with the miserable living conditions in the colony than anything else. It was easy for men to become edgy when life was a constant struggle. Still, while this may explain, it does not excuse Bienville's intransigence. Perhaps, in his final years, he came to realize that he could have spared himself and the colony much grief if he had been more tolerant of dissenting opinion.

One question frequently raised about a government official is whether he used his office for private gain. Certainly Bienville underwent a fair share of denunciations on that score. But if allegations of corruption were enough to bring French colonial officials to trial, almost everyone would have been on trial most of the time. In Bienville's case, even though nothing was ever proved against him, there are enough charges to inspire certain doubts. Very likely he felt justified in allowing himself some perks, at least in his early years of office, considering the hardships he had to endure, and the extra expenses that he was often forced to incur out of his own pocket—he would have been a very unusual man if he did not. But he was a not a man to pillage the colony in order to feather his own nest. He was known to give wine and food to the sick and the indigent out of his own stock, and though he never lived or entertained at all extravagantly as his successor did, he was expected to keep up appearances and to impress the Indians with the might and dignity of the French nation, even when his salary barely topped 1,000 *livres* a year.

Paradoxically, considering his reputation as a man who could be difficult to get along with, Bienville's greatest asset to the colony was his Indian diplomacy. Louisiana would hardly have survived as long as it did without a man who had such prestige among them. He made it his business to learn their likes and dislikes and he never made the mistake of underestimating their intelligence. Even if deep down he had the European's belief in the superiority of the white race, he dealt with the natives in such a way as to gain their respect and admiration, and he insisted that the French treat them properly. Le Page Du Pratz, never a particular admirer of Bienville, gives him his due in this regard. After an argument with an Indian, Du Pratz remarked to Bienville that the Indians were like beasts. The governor answered, he reported, that Du Pratz did not yet know the natives and that when he did he would do them more justice. To be sure, Bienville was not above manipulating the Indians for his own ends—like the time he encouraged a friendly tribe to take prisoners from their enemies, after which he himself returned the prisoners to their homeland as a show of even-handedness. But his aim was always to promote peace. Unfortunately the Natchez War and its aftermath set in motion a chain of events which drove him to the ultimate step, an all-out war against the Chickasaws, which he had managed to avoid for years.

Bienville never received the recognition he deserved for his lifetime of struggle and service. In part he was the victim of his own early success. Because he managed to keep the French flag flying in Louisiana without any spectacular derring-do on his part, the government tended to take his achievements for granted. Soon his name was swept away in the tide of history that saw Louisiana handed over to Spain, then briefly back to France, until it was sold to the United States in 1803. But the Indians did not soon forget him. Long after his departure, they continued to mention him in their speeches to successive governors. French officer Jean-Bernard Bossu tells of a visit he paid to the Alabamans in 1759. "As soon as they saw me they inquired after him [Bienville] and I answered that he was in the great village of Paris in good health, at which they were highly pleased," he relates. "His name is so deeply rooted in the hearts of these good people that his memory will always be dear to them."[1] Today, Bienville's most enduring monument is the city of New Orleans, which protected the soft underbelly of the continent from foreign intrusion and still remains a center of French culture.

[1]Jean-Bernard Bossu, *Travels in the Interior of North America, 1701-62*. Edited and translated by Seymour Feiler. (Norman, Okla., 1962), 174.

Appendix

CHRONOLOGY OF THE MAJOR EVENTS IN BIENVILLE'S LIFE

- 1680 Born in Montreal. Enters the Navy as midshipman at age 12. Later serves under his brother Iberville in Newfoundland and Hudson Bay, where he is wounded in action.

- 1698 Accompanies Iberville to France. King Louis XIV decides to send Iberville to the mouth of the Mississippi to select a site for a possible settlement. Bienville joins the expedition which leaves France in October 1698.

- 1699 The fleet reaches the Mississippi River. For the next 3 years, Bienville helps to select the sites for Fort Maurepas, Fort Mississippi, and Fort Louis at Mobile. He explores the coast line and the interior, makes alliances with Indian tribes, and learns their language.

- 1700 At a place which became known as English Turn, he encounters an English corvette and obliges the captain to turn back.

- 1701 On the death of Commandant Sauvolle, the 21-year-old Bienville assumes command of the colony. Iberville confirms him in this role the following year.

- 1702 Bienville's first administration begins. By dint of diplomacy and diligence, he manages to maintain friendly relations with the Indians, avert attacks by the Carolinians, and hold the poor colony together.

- 1708 Accusations of Bienville's authoritarianism and profiteering having reached the French government, a commissioner named Martin Dartaguiette is sent to Louisiana to investigate the charges. The ensuing trial largely exonerates him.

- 1710 When the settlers are forced to leave their sodden lands at Fort Louis, Mobile, Bienville organizes a new settlement on the site of the present Mobile, Alabama.

- 1713 Bienville's first administration ends with the arrival of Cadillac as governor. The colony is also ceded to financier Antoine Crozat for 15 years in return for developing the population and resources.

- 1714 Bienville is given military command of the Mississippi River from the Ohio to the Gulf of Mexico.

- 1716 Bienville averts a potential war with the Natchez. Later that year, Cadillac is recalled mainly for his bumbling treatment of the Indians.

- 1717 Crozat relinquishes his monopoly which is bestowed on John Law's Company of the West (later the Company of the Indies).

- 1718 Bienville's second administration begins with word of his appointment as Commandant General. He also receives the Cross of St. Louis for his services. Later that year he selects the site for the new capital at New Orleans.

- 1720 John Law's Company goes bankrupt. By the time the news reaches Louisiana, hordes of settlers and slaves are still stranded at the coast awaiting transport upriver. Many perish from disease and hunger. Bienville is held to blame for the debacle.

- 1722 Shifting sands and a little dredging make the river passable for most vessels. Bienville moves his residence to New Orleans, which becomes the capital in fact as well as in name.

- 1723 The re-organized Company decides to recall Bienville for discussions about the colony.

- 1724 Bienville receives his orders to return to France. His cousin Boisbriant is appointed temporary commandant.

- 1725 Bienville and his brother Chateauguay arrive in France. Bienville presents a lengthy memoir to the directors which is severely critical of company methods and policies. He receives a pension of 3,000 *livres* a year from the king, but no official appointments for seven years.

- 1726/ 1732 Étienne Perier, a Company employee, holds command. An all-out war against the Natchez devastates the colony. The Company cedes Louisiana back to the Crown.

- 1732 Bienville is appointed governor.

- 1736 Repeated efforts to bring the Chickasaws to the peace table having failed, Bienville leads an unsuccessful campaign against them.

- 1740 A second campaign against the Chickasaws falls short of expectations. When the enemy sues for peace, Bienville accepts their offer.

- 1741 Bienville begs the minister of the marine for leave to return to France for the good of his health. In the meantime he does his best to pave the way for his successor.

- 1743 The new governor Pierre de Rigaud de Vaudreuil arrives and a few months later Bienville bids a last farewell to Louisiana. For more than twenty years, he lives in retirement in Paris.

- 1767 Bienville dies in Paris.

Bienville's Will

In the name of the Father, etc.

Persuaded, as I am, of the necessity of death, and of the uncertainty of the hour, I wish, before it arrives, to put my affairs in order. Firstly, I consign my soul to God. I wish to live and die in the bosom of the Church. I implore the mercy of God and of Jesus Christ, my Saviour. I ask the protection of the Holy Virgin, Mother of God, and of Saint John the Baptist, my patron saint, and of all the saints of paradise.

I give and bequeath to the poor of the parish in which I die, the sum of one thousand pounds, in one payment. I direct that three hundred masses be said for the repose of my soul, in such church as my testamentary executor may choose. I give and bequeath to the herein-named Verraine, called Picard, my valet, a pension of two hundred and fifty pounds during his life, if he be in my service the day of my death. Moreover, an agreement shall be made with him, by which he shall receive, by the payment of two hundred and fifty pounds, a life rental of the house I placed over his head. I further give and bequeath to him my wardrobe, consisting of all my personal apparel, such as coats, shirts. I further give him the bed and bedding on which he sleeps.

I give and bequeath to the herein-named Renaud, my cook, the sum of three hundred pounds, if she remain in my service till the day of my death.

I give and bequeath to the herein-named Marechal, my footman, two hundred francs, to be paid at once, if he remain in my service till the day of my death.

I give and bequeath to the herein-named Baron, my coachman, the sum of one hundred pounds, if he is still in my service.

I give and bequeath to the herein-named Marguerite, the girl who helps in the kitchen, sixty francs, if she remain in my service till the day of my death.

I declare that all my property is acquired, and that the little which I should have received from my father and mother was lost during my minority; for this reason, being free to dispose of my property in favour of whom I please, I wish by this will, as much as is in my power, to give to all of my nearest relatives marks of my friendship and liberality.

I give and bequeath to my nephew, Payen de Noyan, Siegneur de Chavoy, in lower Normandy, son of my sister Le Moyne de Noyan the sum of ten thousand pounds, to be taken from the share of my grand-nephew, Payen de Noyan, to whom I advanced a like sum of ten thousand pounds to buy a commission in the cavalry, and whose note I hold.

I give and bequeath to my nephew Le Moyne de Longueuil, son of my eldest brother, Le Moyne de Longueuil, a diamond worth fifteen hundred francs, to be paid at once.

I give and bequeath to my two grand-nieces, De Grandive de Lavanaie who are daughters of my niece Le Moyne d'Iberville, who was daughter of my brother Le Moyne d'Iberville, each a diamond worth fifteen hundred pounds.

I make and institute my universal legatees for one fourth, my grand-nephew Le Moyne de Longueuil, son of my nephew Le Moyne de Longueuil, who is son of my eldest brother Le Moyne de Longueuil; my nephew Le Moyne de Sérigny, younger son of my brother Le Moyne de Sérigny, for another fourth. My nephew Le Moyne de Chateauguay, who is the son of my brother Le Moyne de Chateauguay for another fourth. And my grand-nephews Le Moyne de Sérigny de Loire, and their sister, children of my nephew, Le Moyne de Sérigny de Loire, for the last fourth.

I charge my said universal legatees to pay all my just debts, should I leave any,—I do not think I shall,—and to carry out all the provisions of this my present will.

I name as executor of this will my said nephew Le Moyne de Sérigny, younger son of my brother Le Moyne de Sérigny, praying and desiring him to execute my present will as containing my last wishes. To this end I revoke all other wills and codicils, this present one containing my last wishes.

Made, written and signed by my hand in Paris the fifteenth of January, one thousand seven hundred and sixty-five.

LE MOYNE DE BIENVILLE

On the margin:-

Registered in Paris, the fifteenth of April, one thousand seven hundred and sixty-seven.

Received: sixty-five pounds.—LANGLOIS.

I have forgotten in this will to make mention of my nephew Payen de Noyan, son of my sister Le Moyne de Noyan, to whom I give and bequeath a diamond worth fifteen hundred pounds.

Paris, the fifteenth of April, one thousand seven hundred and sixty-five.

LE MOYNE DE BIENVILLE

Registered in Paris, April fifteenth, seventeen hundred and sixty-seven.

Received: thirteen cents.—LANGLOIS.

Bibliographic Essay

In order to make the biography more accessible to the general public, for whom it is intended, I have refrained from encumbering the text with notes, except in the case of actual quotations.

The book is based mainly on printed primary sources in the French language or in translation. Secondary sources were used to provide background information and a better understanding of place and period. Other such sources were consulted to illuminate a particular period or specific event.

Primary Sources

From the Mississippi Provincial Archives we have a wealth of documents covering Bienville's career and the colonization, development, and government of French Louisiana. Collected, edited, and translated by Dunbar Rowland and A. G. Sanders, the first books to appear were *Mississippi Provincial Archives: French Dominion,* 3 vols. (Jackson, Miss., 1927-1932). These volumes were followed by *Mississippi Provincial Archives, French Dominion, 1729-1748,* 2 vols., revised and edited by P. K. Galloway (Baton Rouge, 1984). Most of the documents contained in the books are translations of transcripts of originals classified under the group title *Archives du ministère des colonies* (AC 13A). The remainder are from Series B in the same collection.

The first volume in the series covering the period 1729-1740 deals with French-Indian relations, particularly with the Natchez, Choctaw, and Chickasaw nations. The documents in Volume 2 reveal the daily lives of the people, their trials, morals, and customs. A recurring theme throughout is the bickering of officials, clergy, and colonists. Volume 3 contains all previously unpublished documents illuminating Bienville's career in Louisiana from 1704 to 1743. Volumes 4 and 5 supplement the already published materials and complete the documentary history of French Louisiana.

Another valuable source of information is Pierre Margry's *Mémoires et documents: découverts et établissements des français dans l'ouest et dans le sud de l'Amérique septentrionale,* 6 vols. (Paris, 1879-1885). The documents in Volume 4 include Iberville's accounts of his three voyages and exploration. We also see Bienville's emergence as an explorer, leader, and peacemaker. Included in Volume 5 is André Pénigaut's journal of his life in Louisiana, unreliable as to specific names and dates, but brimful of interesting details and anecdotes. Several documents in Volume 6 deal with efforts at opening the Mississippi to large vessels and the eventual founding of New Orleans. Volume 6 recounts further French exploration into the interior, ultimately as far as Santa Fe.

Volume 9 of *Documents Relative to the Colonial History of the State of New York*, 15 vols., edited by E. B. O'Callaghan (Albany, N.Y., 1856-1863) is a haphazard collection of letters and reports from the Paris archives. Covering the period 1631-1744, the collection paints a picture of Anglo-French rivalry in the New World, the efforts by both sides to win over the Indians, and the Indians' own opinions as shown in their speeches. The important roles played by the LeMoyne family are also touched on.

Three other contemporary narratives from men who came to Louisiana at the beginning of the Law regime bear reading: (a) Dumont de Montigny's *Mémoires historiques sur la Louisiane* (Paris, 1753); (b) *The Historical Journal of the Establishment of the French in Louisiana* [attributed to Bénard de La Harpe] (edited and translated by Glenn Conrad, Lafayette: University of Southwestern Louisiana, 1968); and (c) Le Page du Pratz's *History of Louisiana* (Translated from the French with some notes and observations, London, 1774). Bearing in mind that Dumont de Montigny, a ne'er-do-well from a prominent French family heartily disliked Bienville for not treating him as he thought he deserved, the author can be relied on for his keen observation of his surroundings and the activities of the colonists. The La Harpe journal, on the other hand, consistently shows Bienville in a good light. Arranged in brief chronological entries, it covers the history of the colony from its beginning to 1723 when La Harpe returned to France. The Du Pratz history is most valuable for its sympathetic description of the Indians, particularly the Natchez, among whom he lived for several years.

An eyewitness account of a journey to Louisiana appears in historian Pierre F. X. Charlevoix's *Journal of a Voyage to North America,* 2 vols., (London, 1761), a significant and useful picture of Louisiana in the colony after the collapse of the Law enterprise. Volume 2 describes the countryside, the newly-founded settlement of New Orleans, and meetings with local officials, including Bienville. Charlevoix's other great work, *History and Description of New France* (edited and translated by J. G. Shea, Chicago, 1870) can be consulted as a primary and secondary source since the historian makes extensive use of colonial documents.

An antidote to many of the gloomy accounts of life in the colony is contained in the delightful description of New Orleans and its inhabitants contained in *The Letters of Marie-Madeleine Hachard* (translated by M. M. Costa, Laborde Printing Company, 1974). Hachard was one of a group of six Ursuline nuns who came to New Orleans to look after patients in the hospital and set up a school for girls. In a few brief letters she paints a vivid picture of the new capital, its people, and their manners and morals.

hospital and set up a school for girls. In a few brief letters she paints a vivid picture of the new capital, its people, and their manners and morals. Another brief account worthy of mention is *The Journal of Paul du Ru: Missionary Priest to Louisiana* (translated by Ruth L. Butler, Chicago: Caxton Club, 1934). The young Jesuit priest, who came to Louisiana in January 1700 and returned to France in 1702, has interesting observations about life in Biloxi among the motley collection of soldiers, privateers, Canadians, sailors, and the like.

Volumes 65, 68, 69, and 71 of R. G. Thwaite's *The Jesuit Relations and Allied Documents,* 73 vols. (Cleveland, 1896-1901) contain brief but significant information about the life in the colony, the Natchez Rebellion, and the first settlement at Fort Mississippi.

General Secondary Sources

All histories of French Louisiana have been superseded by the detailed scholarly series of Marcel Giraud, *Histoire de la Louisiane française*: Vol. I: *Le reigne de Louis XIV* (Paris: Presses Universitaires de France, 1953); Vol. II: *Les années de transition, 1715-1717* (1958); Vol. III: *Le système de Law, 1717-1720*; Vol. IV: *La Louisiane après le système de Law, 1721-1723*; Vol. V: *La Compagnie des Indies, 1723-1731.* Volumes I and II of the series have been translated into English under the titles, *A History of Louisiana* I and *A History of Louisiana* V (Louisiana State University Press, 1974, 1991). A very trenchant and readable analysis of the often troubled relationship between Church and state may be found in Charles O'Neill's *Church and State in French Colonial Louisiana: Policy and Politics to 1732* (New Haven: Yale University Press, 1966). Also useful, particularly for years leading up to and following the secession is Marc de Villiers du Terrage's, *Les dernières années de la Louisiane française* (Paris: Maisonneuve, 1904). The only biography of Bienville is Grace King's *Jean-Baptiste LeMoyne, Sieur de Bienville* (New York, 1892). Since its publication, new materials have come to light about the man and his era. Worthy of mention also is Nellis Crouse's *LeMoyne d'Iberville, Soldier of New France* (Toronto: Ryerson, 1954). In covering Iberville's career, the author provides background information on the Le Moyne family and touches on Bienville's part in Iberville's campaigns and explorations.

A very useful reference for the study of French-Indian relations is found in Patricia Dillon's *French-Indian Relations on the Southern Frontier, 1699-1762* (Ann Arbor: UMI Research Press, 1980). The role of the Indians in Anglo-French rivalry in the region is also laid out in Verner W. Crane's *The Southern Frontier, 1670-1732* (Durham: Duke University in Louisiana. Included also is Captain de Richbourg's contemporary account of the first Natchez "war."

Other Sources

As well as the works already cited, other sources that were found valuable in the preparation of this study are noted below. The first historian of Montreal, Dollier de Casson gives otherwise unavailable information spiced with colorful anecdotes about the town and its pioneers. For a good translation see Dollier de Casson, *A History of Montreal, 1640-1672* (edited and translated by Ralph Flenley, Toronto: Dent, 1928). Volumes I, II, and III of *The Dictionary of Canadian Biography* (University of Toronto Press, 1969) also provide a basic reference containing biographies of the most notable Le Moynes, including Bienville. Chapters V and VI of *The Canadian Frontier* by W. J. Eccles (Toronto: Holt, Rinehart, & Winston, 1969) are indispensable for an understanding of the forces which influenced Bienville's later attitude and career. For an understanding of the calibre of the governor with whom Bienville had to contend during the Crozat regime, see Jean Delanglez's articles on Cadillac in *Mid America* (XXVII, 1945, 108-132, 188-216, 232-256; XXX, 1948, 75-104, 152-176, 233-256; XXXII, 1950, 155-188, 226-258; XXX, 1951, 3-39, 39-42.

John Law's "system" and the unfortunate aftermath of its collapse, particularly for Louisiana, come alive in James Breck Perkins' *France under the Regency with a Review of the Administration of Louis XIV* (Cambridge, 1892). The best study of events in the Franco-Spanish War is by Jack R. Holmes in *Frenchmen and French Ways in the Mississippi Valley* (edited by John F. McDermott, Urbana: University of Illinois, 1969).

For the ambience and political climate of Louisiana following Bienville's departure, see Guy Fregault's *Le grand marquis, Pierre de Rigaud de Vaudreuil et la Louisiane* (Montreal: Fides Press, 1968) and the contemporary account of his travels written by J. R. Bossu, *Travels in North America, 1751-1762* (translated and edited by Seymour Feiler, 1778, London: Foster).

Index

Ackia, 124, 127
Alabama Indians, 26, 27, 60, 117, 127
Alabama Mingo, 112, 121
Alarcon, Martin de, 77
Alexander VI, 21
Ancient Hair, 98, 100
Apalachee Indians, 30, 36, 53, 89
Apple Village, 98, 99, 100, 109
Arkansas Indians, 27, 30, 91
Arnaud, Sieur, 93
Artus, Sieur d', 65
Aubry, Charles-Philippe, 138

Badine, The, 9, 14
bandoliers of Louisiana, 80
Baron, Jean, 114
Bayogoula Indians, 11, 12, 15
Bayou Manchac, 13, 62
Bayou St. Jean, 15, 69
Beaubois, Nicolas, 105, 106, 135
Beauchamp, 114
Beaudouin, Father, 118, 127
Beauharnois, Charles de la Boische de, 105, 129
Beaujeu, Taneguy Le Gallois de, 24
Belle Isle, Comte de, 80
Bellone, The, 101
Bénard de La Harpe, 37
Béranger, Captain, 72
Bergier, Father, 40
Berneval, Commandant, 98
Bienville, Jean-Baptiste Le Moyne, Sieur de, 10, 107, 108, 109, 110, 113, 115; activities of, to be investigated by DeMuy and Dartaguiette, 43-44; appointed commandant of the Wabash region, 64; as administrator, discussed, 31-32; at Battle of Port Nelson, 8, at Pensacola Bay 9-10; awarded Cross of St. Louis, 66; baptismal date of, 1; becomes navy cadet, 7, commissioned king's lieutenant, 16; Company of the Indies recalls, 100; concern of, for school for boys, 135, decides to intervene in Natchez disturbances, 99; decides route of attack on Chickasaws, 127; education of, 5; embroglio with Nicolas de La Salle, discussed, 40-42; establishes charity hospital, 120; excoriated by La Chaise, 95-96; expedition against the Alabama Indians, 26-27; expedition to the Cenis, 18-19; his career appraised, 139-42; last will and testament of, 137; memoir on conditions in Louisiana, 102-3; Mississippi River expedition, 11-12; orders Capt. Bond to leave the Mississippi, 16; plan to attack Chickasaw Indians, 123; prepares for Second Chickasaw War, 126; promotes Chickasaw-Choctaw harmony, 27-29; relations with Indians, 25, reports on Louisiana upon his return to France, 117-118; strained relations with Father La Vente, 38-40; takes command of Fort Maurepas, 20, the Natchez expedition, 61-63
Bienvillists, 106
Biloxi, 24, 70, 81
Biloxi, New, 69
Biloxi, Old, 69
Biloxi Bay, first French settlement on, 13
Biloxi Indians, 13
Blondel, Corporal, 77
Boisbriant, Pierre Dugué de, 16, 22, 28, 34, 68, 69, 101, 104, 117
Boisrenaud, Marie Françoise, 34
Bonavists, 7
Bond, Captain, 15-16
Bossu, Jean-Bernard, 142
Bourbon, Duc de, 104
Bourgmond, Etienne Véniard de, 78-79
Broutin, Ignace, 108, 114, 126, 130
Bru, Louis, 106
Buslé, Antoine, 92, 96

Cabildo, 139
Caddo Indians, 78
Caddoan Indians, 76
Cadillac, Antoine de La Mothe, 50, 51, 63, 64, 76, 140; background of, 55; opinion of the colony and its people, 56; visits Illinois country, 59
Cadodaquois Indians, 19
Calderon, Gregorio Guazo, 73
Callières, Louis Hector de, 24
Cap Français, 21
Capuchins, 92
Carbonnear, 7
Carolina Galley, The, 15
Carolina, 15, 16, 22, 26, 27
Carolinians, 107, 133; fear growing population of Louisiana, 90; plan renewed attack on Louisiana, 51; seek to make peace with the Choctaws, 29-30; seek to win Indian allegiance, 29-30
Céleron de Blainville, 130, 131
Cenis Indians, 18
Champmeslin, Danos de, 75
charity hospital, 120
Charles III, 138
Charles Town, 26, 28, 133
Charlevoix, Pierre-François-Xavier de, 72, 87, 89
Chateauguay, Antoine Le Moyne de,

16, 22, 30, 64, 68, 69, 72, 73, 74, 75, 89, 95, 101, 104, 106, 117, 137
Chavagnac, Comte de, 25
Chavannes, Jean-Baptiste de, 96
Cherokee Indians, 60
Chickasaw Indians, 14, 18, 22, 24, 26, 51, 52, 54, 90-91, 101, 110, 114, 116, 117, 118, 119, 121, 122, 123, 124, 125, 126, 127, 128, 131, 132, 133, 134, 142; and trade goods, 27-28
Chickasaw War, First, 119
Chocolissa, 123
Choctaw Indians, 18, 21, 22, 24, 26, 27, 28, 30, 51, 52, 54, 59, 60, 89 - 90, 101, 107, 108, 110, 111, 112, 114, 117, 118, 121, 122, 123, 124, 125, 126, 127,128, 129, 131, 132, 134
Choiseul, Comte de, 25
Choiseul, Duc de, 138
Chomedy de Maisonneuve, Paul, founder of Montreal, 3, 5
Chouache Indians, 111, 114
Clairambault d'Aigrement, 55, 64
Colapissa Indians, 14, 15, 78
Company of China, 80
Company of New France, 2
Company of the Indies, 67, 69, 79, 92, 102, 106, 114, 135, 141
Company of the West, 65, 67, 72, 78, 80
Comte de Toulouse, The, 73
Conseil de Marine, 63
Contrecoeur, Chevalier de, 124
Council of Commerce, 68
Council of Commerce, 85
Coustilhas, Jacques de, 128
Coxe, Daniel, 8, 16
Creek Indians, 26, 51-52, 60
Cresnay, Baron de, 113
Crozat, Antoine, 50, 61, 63, 65, 68; monopoly of, unfavorable for colonists, 57

D"Abbadie, Jean-Jacques, 138
D'Arensbourg, Captain, 97
Darrac, 78
Dartaguiette, Diron, 106, 107, 108, 111, 114, 119, 121, 122
Dartaguiette, Martin, 43, 106; investigates the Le Moynes, 45-46, 47, 48, 49, 51
Dartaguiette, Pierre, 112, 123, 124, 130
D'Assigny, Gabriel, 21
Dauphin Island, 22, 24, 53, 68, 69, 71, 72, 73, 74, 75, 76, 101; English attack on, 49
Dauseville, Raymond, 106
Davion, Antoine, 15, 37, 62, 92, 94
De Batz, Alexandre M., 127
De Blanc, Captain, 97
De Léry, Joseph Chauvin *dit*, 127
De Muy, Nicolas Daneau, 43, 45, 141
Delay, Jean-François, 112
Delorme, 85, 88, 93, 95, 114
Desliettes, Charles, 99
Detchéparre, Captain, 108, 109, 110, 114
Dodun, Charles-Gaspard, 102, 104
Dollier de Casson, 4
Dongé, Father, 36
Douay, Anastas, 9, 11, 12, 13
Ducasse, Jean-Baptiste, 24
Duchesne, Adrien, 2
Duclos, Jean-Baptiste, 50, 55-56, 57, 63, 64
Dumont de Montigny, 96
Du Ru, Paul, 16, 17, 20
Du Tisné, Claude-Charles, 78, 98
Duval, François, 97
Duvergier, Michel-Léon, 85, 95

East Indian Company, 80
English colonies, reaction of, to French-Chicasaw War, 127-28
English Turn, 15
epidemic, at New Orleans, 94

Fazende, Jacques, 92, 106
Ferryland, 7
Fontaine, Sergeant, 97
Fontenac, Louis de Buade, comte de, 4-5
Fort Assumption, 128, 130, 131
Fort Charlotte, 137
Fort Chartres, 123, 135, 137
Fort Condé, 89, 106, 126, 137
Fort Crèvecoeur, 72
Fort d'Orléans, 79
Fort de La Boulaye, 17, 19, 69
Fort Detroit, 50
Fort Louis de la Mobile, 40, 49; described, 22
Fort Maurepas, 15, 19, 20; construction of, 13-14
Fort Mississippi, see Fort de La Boulaye
Fort Prudhomme, 123
Fort Rosalie, 63, 91, 97, 98, 99, 108, 113
Fort-St.-Louis, 76
Fort St. Pierre, 91
Fort Tombigbee, 123, 134, 137
Fort Toulouse, 65, 87, 137
Foucault, Denis-Nicolas, 138
Foucault, Father, 27, 37
Fox Indians, 79
French and Indian War, 137
French-Spanish relations, discussed, 52-53
Froebel, Sieur, 88
Frontenac, 38, 55

Galatée, The, 93
Garonne, The, 116
German Coast, 84
German settlers, 83-84

girls, brought to Louisiana to marry, 34-35
Gironde, The, 79, 101
Gravier, Jacques, 17, 19, 42, serves as military chaplain at Fort Louis, 40
Great Sun, 108, 109, 110
Grisot, Marie, 49
Guenot, Captain, 97, 98
Guilhet, Antoine, 93
Guzman, Governor, 35

Hastings, Theophilis, 51-52
Houalt de Montmagny, 3
Houma Indians, 12, 15
Hubert, Marc-Antoine, 63, 65, 68, 70, 80, 81, 85, 95, 97, 100
Huché, Antoine, 90
Hughes, Price, 59
Huguenots, 16
Huronia, 2
Huvé, Father, 42, 89

Iberville, Pierre Le Moyne, Sieur d' 7, 11, 19, 20, 27, 38, 41,60, 69, 76, 107, 111, 140; arrives at Mobile Bay, 10; at Pensacola Bay, 9-10; conducts negotiations between Chickasaw and Choctaw Indians, 22-23; death of, 23; lays out Mobile, 22; leads French at Battle of Port Nelson; leaves Louisiana for France, 19; Mississippi River expedition, 11-13; proposes establishing a post at Mobile, 21, returns to Biloxi Bay, 16
Illinois Indians, 79, 129
Iowa Indians, 79
Iroquois Indians, attacks on Montreal, 3

Jesuits, 36, 107, 140
Johnson, Robert, 90

Kansas Indians, 79
Kolly, Mrs., 121
Koroa Indians, 12, 27, 30

La Chaise, Jacques de, 92, 93, 94, 95, 96, 97, 100, 102, 106, 107, 114; excoriates Bienville, 95-96
Lafrénière, Nicolas Chauvin de, 138
La Harpe, Bénard de, 71, 72, 77, 78, 91
Lake Maurepas, 13, 15, 62
Lake Pontchartrain, 13, 15, 62, 69, 70, 80
LaMothe, Madeleine, 64
Larcebault, 73, 95
La Riola, Andrés de, 10
La Salle, Nicolas de, 21, 22, 31, 32, 34, 35, 40, 45, 46, 47, 56, 140; embroglio with Bienville, discussed, 40-42
La Salle, René-Robert Cavelier de, 8, 9, 11, 13, 17, 18, 24, 41, 72, 76
Lavaca River, 76
La Vente, Roullaux de, 36, 42, 43, 46, 47, 48, 140; discussed, 37-38
Law, John, 65, 67, 80, 140; collapse of "system," 82; concessions, 80
Le Blanc, Claude, 80
Leblond de La Tour, 81, 83, 88, 94, 98, 99, 101
Le Brie, 26
Le Gac, Charles, 70, 81, 95
Le Maire, Father, 45, 70
Le Moyne, Charles, 1, 2-3, 4; birth of, 2; death of, 4
Le Moyne, Jacques, 2
Le Moyne d'Iberville, Pierre, see Iberville
Le Moyne de Bienville, Jean-Baptiste, see Bienville
Le Moyne de Saint-Hélène, 7
Leon, Alonso de, 76
Le Page du Pratz, 71, 73, 97, 99, 109, 142
Lépinay, Jean-Michel de, 63, 65, 140
Lescalette, Lieutenant, 9, 10
Le Sueur, Pierre Charles, 16, 17, 20, 22, 111, 112, 119, 121
Le Vasseur, Charles, 22
Limoges, Joseph de, 20
Loire des Ursins, Marc-Antoine de, 59, 106
Longueuil et de Chateauguay, Sieur de (see also Le Moyne, Charles), 2
Longueuil, 137
Longueuil, Baron de, 64, 105, 129, 130
Los Adais, 76, 77, 78
Louboey, Henry de, 93, 111, 112, 113, 117, 119, 129
Louis XIV, 8, 10, 16, 21, 42, 63, 79
Louis XV, 138
Louis, Jean, 120
Louisiana, Bienville's memoir on conditions in, 102-3; depiction of, 68, divided into nine military districts, 85; living conditions in, 33-34; social conditions in, 86-87; trade possibilities in, 121
Lusser, Joseph de, 124

Macarty, Major, 116
Maisonneuve, see Chomedy de Maisonneuve
Mallet, Paul, 135
Mallet, Pierre, 135
Mandieta, Captain, 75
Marchand de Courcelles, 87
Maréchal de Villars, The, 73
Marin, The, 9, 14
marriage, French-Indian, 39
Marsillo, Father, 77
Martinez, Francisco, 21
Martinique, 134

Masclary, Sieur, 92, 93
Massacre Island (see also Dauphin Island), 10
Matagorda Bay, 17
Matamores de Isla, Governor, 73
Maurepas, Jean Frédéric Phélypeaux, Comte de, 102, 115, 116, 119, 120, 121, 124, 126, 128, 132, 135, 136
Membré, Zénobe, 9
Membrède, Jean Baptiste de, 126
Mendoza, Gaspar Domingo de, 135
Merveilleux, François-Louis de, 111
Milhet, Jean, 138
military districts, Louisiana divided into nine, 85
Missouri River, 78
Mobile, 15, 21, 24, 26, 30, 32, 34, 36, 37, 50, 69, 74, 76, 89, 107
Mobile Indians, 26, 30
Moctoby Indians, 13
Monceaux, Sieur, 46
Montigny, François-Jolliet de, 15, 20
Moore, James, 26
Mugulasha Indians, 11, 12

Nairne, Thomas, 29
Nakasi Indians, 19
Natchez incident, 97-100
Natchez Indians, 30, 60, 62, 91, 99, 108-14, 116, 122, 123
Natchez post, 61
Natchez War, 108-14, 142
Natchitoches, 63, 77, 78, 113
Natchitoches Indians, 19, 57, 129
New Biloxi, 82
New Orleans, 69, 70, 71, epidemic in, 94; laid out, 88
Nouailles d'Ayme, Louis de, 130, 131, 132, 133
Noyan, Bienville, 138
Noyan, Chevalier de, 113
Noyan, Jean-Baptiste de, 138

O'Reilly, Alejandro, 138
Orléans, Duc d' (see also Prince Regent), 63, 65, 79
Orry, Philibert d', 114, 115
Osage Indians, 78, 79
Oto Indians, 79

Padouca Indians, 78, 79
Pailloux, 46, 63, 70, 88, 97, 98
Paris-Duverney, Joseph, 80
Pascagoula Indians, 13, 26, 30, 74
Pauger, Adrien de, 82, 88
Pawnee Indians, 78, 79
Pax Gallica, 23
Payen de Noyan, 117
Payen de Noyan, Gilles-Augustin, 74, 105
Payen de Noyan, Pierre Benoit, 124, 128
Pelican, The, 7
Pénigaut, André, 16, 35, 36
Pensacola, 15, 21, 30, 52, 53, 72, 79, 89, 140; Carolinians plan attack on, 45; French attack on, 73-75; retaken by the French, 75
Pensacola Indians, 30
Perault, 106
Périer, Etienne de, 96, 104, 106, 107, 108, 111, 113, 114, 115, 116, 117, 118
Périer de Salvert, 111, 113
Perrier, Etienne, 70, 81
Perry, Paul, 92, 93, 106
Petit Michel, 23, 28
Philibert, Father, 109, 110
Philippe, The, 75
Phipps, William, 7
Point St. Antoine, 80
Poisson, Father, 110
Pontchartrain, Jérôme Phélypeaux de Maurepas, comte de Pontchartrain, 13, 17, 24, 32, 33, 34, 35, 38, 40, 42, 43, 45, 47, 50, 52, 53, 55, 56, 59, 61, 63, 64, 104
Port Dauphin, 54
Port Nelson, 7; battle of, 8
Pradel, Chevalier de, 134
Presidio de San Juan Bautista, 57
Primot, Catherine, 4
Prince Regent (see also Orléans, Duc d'), 67, 69, 72, 76, 80, 82, 84, 89, 92, 102
Profond, The, 7
Prudhomme Bluffs, 126

Raguet, Jean-Baptiste, 95
Raphael, Father, 95, 106, 135
Red River, 18
Red Shoe, 119, 121, 124, 125, 128, 129
Renommé, The, 46
Richebourg, Captain, 73
Ritter, Sergeant, 91
Roullet, Régis de, 107

Saint Augustine, 133
Saint Bernard's Bay, 72
Saint Catherine Concession, 97, 98, 99, 100
Saint Cosme, Father, 32, 116
Saint Denis, Louis Juchereau de, 16, 18, 26, 48, 57, 63, 74, 76, 77, 78, 77, 113
Saint Francis River, 127, 128, 130
Saint Hélène, Jacques Le Moyne de, 7, 48
Saint Joseph's Bay, 72
Saint Louis de Biloxi, 82
Saint, Vallier, Bishop, 34, 36
Salmon, Edme, 114, 119, 120, 121, 127, 133, 135
San Miguel de Linares de los Adais, 76
Santa Fe, 78, 135
Saucier, François, 128, 130
Sauvolle, 9, 11, 13, 16, 20; in charge of

Fort Maurepas, 19
Sauvoy, 92, 93, 94
Seminary of the Foreign Missions, 15, 36, 37
Senat, Father, 123
Sérigny, Joseph Le Moyne de, 7, 8, 17, 21, 22, 23, 25, 41, 73, 74, 75, 104, 137
settlers, condition of, 82-83
Seven Years' War, 137
Ship Island, 15, 72, 81, 93; anchorage at, 10
slavery, black and Indian, discussed, 47
soldiers, conditions of, 48-49
Souchonino Indians, 19
Spanish-French relations, discussed, 52-53
Stung Serpent, 98, 99, 108, 109
Superior Council, 99, 139
Surgères, Chevalier de, 9, 11

Tamaroa Indians, 37
Tensas Indians, 30
Texarkana, 77
Thierry, Catherine, 1; death of, 4
Thomé Indians, 26, 30, 59
Tombigbee, River, 126
Tonty, Henry de, 12, 13, 17, 18, 20, 22, 26, 34
Toulouse, Comte de, 63, 65
Treaty of Paris, 137
Treaty of Utrecht, 59
Trinity River, 76
Trudeau, François, 74
Tunica Indians, 30, 37, 62, 111, 112, 113

Ulloa, Antonio de, 138
Unzaga, Luis de, 139
Ursuline nuns, 107, 120-21

Valigny, Sieur de, 46
Vaudreuil, Pierre de Rigaud, Marquis de, 136
Vera Cruz, 21, 30, 54, 75, 76
Verges, Bernard de, 126, 127, 128, 133
Villanville, Sieur, 75
Villardeau, 75, 95
Vitry, Pierre de, 128

War of the Quadruple Alliance, 71, 73, 76
War of the Spanish Succession, 23, 24, 50, 52, 59, 106
wax myrtle, 134
Welch, Thomas, 29, 30, 52
White Earth Concession, 97
Wichita Indians, 19, 78
Yamasee War, 59-60, 90
Yatasi Indians, 19
Yazoo Indians, 30
Yazoo Post, 110
Yomani, 28